THE
GODS OF
ANTENNA

THE GODS OF ANTENNA

BRUCE HERSCHENSOHN

ARLINGTON HOUSE·PUBLISHERS
NEW ROCHELLE, N. Y.

Manufactured in the United States of America

Library of Congress Cataloging in Publication Data

Herschensohn, Bruce.
  The gods of antenna.

  Includes index.
  1. Mass media—United States. 2. Nixon,
Richard Milhaus, 1913-   I. Title.
P92.U5H38   301.16'1   75-32403
ISBN 0-87000-346-1

Contents

Dedicated to Dr. Herbert L. Herschensohn and Mrs. Ida E. Herschensohn who, most fortunately for me, are my parents.

If I live one thousand years there will still not be time enough to give to them all they have given me.

Prologue: A Crowd, a Podium, and Tears

There was a crowd, a podium, and tears. When something good is over and done and its termination is made public, there is always a crowd, a podium, and tears. And something very good was over and done.

It was the last day of his administration and he gave his final speech as President of the United States. Those who supported him and fought for him and worked for him wept publicly and had no shame in crying.

As they listened to him speak, the newspaper that had most vilified him since he came to office was printing its final editorial regarding his administration:

> The man who is the source of all misfortunes of our country is this day reduced to a level with his fellow citizens, and is no longer possessed of power to multiply evils upon the United States. If ever there was a period for rejoicing, this is the moment. Every heart in unison with the freedom and happiness of the people ought to beat high with exultaion that his name ceases from this day to give currency to political insults, and to legalize corruption. A new era is now opening upon us, an era which promises much to the people, for public measures must now stand upon their own merits, and nefarious projects can no longer be supported by a name. When a retrospect has been taken of his administration, it is a subject of the greatest astonishment that a single individual should have cankered the principles of republicanism in an enlightened people, and

should have carried his designs against the public liberty so far as to have put in jeopardy its very existence. Such, however, are the facts, and with these staring us in the face, the day ought to be a jubilee in the United States.

After reading the editorial, former President George Washington went to his native Virginia, with the hope of living his remaining days in peace at Mount Vernon.

Among other charges, he had been accused of overdrawing his salary while in office, stealing thousands of dollars, and of isolating himself from the people, "given to the seclusion of a monk and the supercilious distance of a tyrant." President Washington had called the charges of the press "the most willful, artful and malignant misrepresentations that can be imagined," meant to "weaken, if not destroy, the confidence of the public." He termed their accusations "outrages on common decency."

But that was a long time ago.

The full potential of a communication medium to demoralize, to distort, and to destroy was not even a glimmer on the American horizon at Washington's Farewell. After fighting against the non-elected power and tyranny of King George III, those who achieved the revolution and formed the nation and wrote the Constitution could not possibly have foreseen the day when a multichrome moving visual image would have the power to influence the nation beyond the branches of government that had been so painstakingly established in coequality.

But that day was to come.

Images that could move, but if vivisected would be found to have neither heart nor soul, were in two centuries' time to become everything but the reincarnation of the king from whom the independence-seekers had severed all bonds.

A Lion
Is Dead in Culver City

Fifty-one years after Washington's Farewell and more than a century before the fall of Agnew and the fall of Nixon and the fall of Cambodia and the fall of South Vietnam and the fall of Laos, a child was born in New Jersey who looked very much like Mickey Rooney.

He was not Mickey Rooney.

He was Young Tom Edison who, upon growing up to be Edison the Man, bore an incredible resemblance to Spencer Tracy, which was very convenient.

It is doubtful that either Young Tom Edison or Edison the Man ever heard of the Agnews of Baltimore, the Nixons of Yorba Linda, the Lons of Preyveng, the Nguyens of Ninh Thuan, or the Bounkhongs of Luang Prabang, yet he was to have a striking impact upon their descendants, all of whom were to be fallen leaders within 20 months of one another.

He didn't mean to do it. He started the whole thing in innocence. It was meant to be a toy, not a revolutionary device. He called it the kinetoscope, he exhibited it to the public, and then he went back to more serious things.

The kinetoscope flickered its visual images and people were transfixed as they watched pictures of horses that really looked as though they were running. Then the images were projected on a screen and a man flickered at 16 frames a second and sneezed and audiences laughed because

11

he sneezed. Then an organ played in the pit of an exhibition hall for those moving images as what appeared to be fire engines raced from the left of the screen to the right of the screen and back from the right to the left, and the audience was frightened. Then a man with a long mustache tied a pretty girl to railroad tracks, and the audience hissed and booed. Then a man on the screen knelt and sang, and the audience heard his voice, and it was amazing. Then the images changed from black-and-white to color.

As this was going on, a Scotsman named John Baird, who in no way resembled a movie star at all, thought of a way to bring moving visual images into homes. At the time, no one paid any attention to him.

Motion picture theaters provided an immediate diversion from day-to-day life. From the end of the 1930s and into the early 1940s, people stood in Saturday night lines in front of the Sherman Theater in Milwaukee, the Loma in San Diego, and Loew's in New York City. And they entered those theaters for their two or three hours of escape in front of the silver screen.

Motion pictures told Hollywood-produced stories about love and war and singers and gangsters and millionaires and cowboys, and they gave their American audiences a telescopic view of the rest of the world: Africa was a continent of headhunters, wild animals, and Johnny Weissmuller. Latin America was Carmen Miranda, the rhumba, and a chihuahua in the arms of Xavier Cugat. India was elephants, cobras, and Sabu. The Mid-East was sand dunes, camels, and Dennis Morgan. And the Far East was chopsticks, hara-kiri, and Keye Luke.

There was distortion beyond comprehension, but no one cared. No pickets. No demonstrations. No citizens' groups. The screen was erected for diversion, entertainment, and for box office.

Occasionally an artist would come along: a painter of sorts who saw the screen as a giant canvas. His paints could consist of moving men and women and great literature and music and dance and the locales of times past and present. He could be a creator utilizing a mix of all art forms and, once his creation was complete, it could be exhibited for millions simultaneously, and its value could surpass diversion and entertainment and box office. And so the screen progressed; while some films were mediocre and some were less than mediocre, some were magnificent.

So it went through those years. Then, with the end of World War II, Baird's invention of 20 years before was reexamined and improved. As the 1950s began, his invention caught on, and little screens emerged in living rooms, then wider screens were built in theaters to compete with those little screens that had emerged in living rooms. The moving visual image was competing for prime time in the lives of human beings. Books that would have been read weren't read. Conversations that would have taken place didn't take place. Deeds and misdeeds that would have been done weren't done. The most valuable commodity of human life—time —was increasingly spent in front of a screen.

After the proliferation of television, combined with the continuance of the theater, the average 18-year-old had spent 12,000 hours in school and 15,500 hours in front of a screen. The screen took first place over studies, over friends, over parents, and well over the printed word. What the screen said, what images it portrayed, what moral and political obligation or lack of moral and political obligation it prescribed for itself became of tremendous consequence.

A sneezing man would hardly suffice anymore. The screen was a serious device with a vast power and vast responsibilities of its own.

Post-World War II theatrical screens were becoming the mirror of their times with such productions as "Crossfire," "Gentlemen's Agreement," and "Pinky."

Then came "Rebel Without A Cause." It was a beautifully creative achievement of the 1950s, a magnificent motion picture. And it was more than that. It was the first antiestablishment film that pinpointed and "heroized" youth, and its effect upon the young was tremendous. By this single film, young people achieved at once equal stature and recognition with those twice their age. But the title told it all, and the irony in real life of James Dean, who was the film's lead, dying without a cause created a temporary legend.

The young felt they needed a cause.

They found one.

Civil Rights.

Many young people focused on that national disease. In large part, they were responsible for pursuing and starting to correct the horror of prejudice.

What was the next cause?

The screen was espousing one.

The early 1960s saw a new brand of motion picture. In rapid succession film-making creativity and artistry at its highest produced "On The Beach," "Dr. Strangelove," "Fail Safe," "The Manchurian Candidate," and "Seven Days in May."

Those films had one common denominator. Their screenplay writers dealt with neither the past nor the present: they dealt with a projection of the future. By so doing, they captured the imaginations of the young, who saw those films as a forecast of what could happen during *their* time

13

on earth. The prophecy was the probability of doom. The culprit? The U.S. military-political coalition. Adults who saw the films and who had lived through the war years and those who had served in the military were merely entertained. But the young who did not know the American military were not merely entertained. The film-makers' talent, wit, creativity, humor, pseudoreality, identification, and relevance made those films into frightening nightmares of prophecy. Their collective image adversely affected the credibility and, later, even the ability of the military to function effectively.

That was not the end of it. That was the beginning of it.

The mid-1960s arrived with the biggest entertainment surprise of all, but some didn't notice because it wasn't an isolated event. The surprise was the screen, the mirror of the times. It warped and bulged like the mirror in the fun house of an amusement park, reflecting images out of proportion— too thin in one place, too fat in another.

That alone would not have been harmful, not even worth talking about years before when people watched the screens for a diversion and an escape at the Sherman Theater in Milwaukee, the Loma in San Diego, and Loew's in New York City.

But in the mid-1960s they watched the screens for both diversion and knowledge, and old and young watched them not only at the Sherman, Loma, and Loew's, but at the New Chox in Dar es Salaam, the Palace in Karachi, The Presidente in Guayaquil, and they watched screens in the living rooms of Stockholm, Caracas, and Hong Kong. Those screens created a composite picture of the United States. While American youth became disenchanted with their country through these images on the screen, the foreign audience was both shocked and relieved that "America is not so great."

People in foreign lands were making judgments on American society. Those judgments were based not so much on our official statements or the rich American woman they met at the Hilton or the loud American man in the funny sport shirt with all the cameras, as their estimates had often been made in years past. In the mid-1960s they could see what appeared to be an authentic cross–section of the United States as often as they wished, without chance meetings and without ever leaving their own borders. They could make so-called educated judgments on our capacity of leadership, our compassion or selfishness, our morality or immorality, and our self-discipline or abandon. Their judgments were made by watching screens. All different kinds of screens. Glass screens in living rooms. Beaded screens in meeting halls. Wide and curved screens in theaters. Both the foreign citizen and the young citizen of America were receiving messages of negativism, without anything to offer an educated counterbalance. The imbalanced messages became more intense as the 1970s arrived.

They saw films that portrayed American youth: "Getting Straight" or "The Revolutionary," for example. But those films didn't portray a majority of the country's youth. How could the foreign audience or the young American audience know that?

They saw films that portrayed American race relations: "The Liberation of L.B. Jones" or "Putney Swope," for example. But those films didn't portray the civil rights story of the country. How could the foreign audience or the young American audience know that?

They saw films that portrayed the American military: "M.A.S.H." or "Soldier Blue," for example. But those films didn't portray a realistic picture of the thinking of the American military. How could the foreign audience or the young American audience know that?

They saw films that portrayed the United States in general: "Who's That Knocking At My Door?" or "Easy Rider," for example. But those films didn't portray the feelings of most Americans. How could the foreign audience or the young American audience know that?

Did they see on their screens the same United States of America that they could have seen by traveling throughout the 50 states?

No.

In the politically oriented films of the early 1970s, the images seen were the images of protest. The giant studios of Hollywood, which had so often been accused of rejecting new talent and stifling creativity, were overtaken. But the revolutionaries brought liabilities to rest beside their assets. Like Castro for Batista, the exchange was not so noble as its first signs indicated. They killed the lion and became the vulture.

The antiestablishment of film making had, in the early 1970s, become the establishment, but it didn't want to be recognized as such lest it no longer be considered the underdog, crying for a voice.

Look for a film made in those days that satirized the government. There were many. Look for a film that praised it. There were few, if any.

Look for a film that ridiculed the police. There were many. Look for a film that praised them. There were few, if any.

Look for a film that condemned American society in general. There were many. Look for a film that complimented American society in general. There were few, if any.

Look for a film that criticized America's Vietnam policy. There were many. Look for a film that praised it. There was one.

The United States was as misrepresented on the serious screens of the early 1970s as other countries had been misrepresented on the fun screens of the early 1930s and the 1940s.

15

Simultaneously parallel with the history of American films, the Soviet Union rewarded its own motion picture creators as highly paid government servants. And without exception they all served the government.

Film Festivals in Iron Curtain countries were accepted first as political events and second as exhibitions of creativity.

When motion pictures were no more than an infant, Lenin had said, "Of all the arts, for us the most important one is the cinema."

In the 1950s Stalin said, "The cinema is the greatest means of mass agitation. The task is to take it into our hands. If I could control the medium of the motion pictures I would need nothing else in order to convert the entire world to communism in a very few years."

In the 1960s, Khrushchev stated, "By its force of influencing the feelings and minds of the people and by its scope of reaching the broadest masses of the people, nothing can compare with the art of the cinema."

They were right, of course. In this case the ally of a closed society was a free society. The most credible anti-American messages were produced within the United States by United States film makers.

Was all of this American-made cinematic criticism and ridicule of our country meant to be harmful to the country? Some was. But most of the films were made by well-intentioned American film-makers who wanted to say something valuable through their own creativity. They used creativity to advance a cause, which is the highest art. Although their motivation was not malicious, except for a few, their effect was eroding world opinion of America and propagating cynicism in the youngest Americans.

Fiction was interpreted as fact. Giant canvasses evoked emotion, as canvasses are meant to do. But emotion does not always rest its case on logic.

The unhappy fact was not that artists with a cause utilized their creativity for that cause, but that too many artists with a positive view of the country did not awaken to the power of the screen. Diverse views were virtually nonexistent.

It started in innocence. It was a toy. It wasn't meant to be anything else. But it didn't remain a toy. It became an art form, and that was worthwhile, and it became an international influence and that was a risk requiring the highest degree of responsibility and diversity. Its impact increased tenfold as television became the instrument of motion pictures replayed and new premieres and news reporting. The moving visual image became our key bridge to knowledge and lack of knowledge.

For good or ill the moving visual image, which was the mirror of our times, was fast becoming the maker of our times.

2

A Wife, Two Children, and a 21-Inch Philco

and Thank God They are All in Perfect Health

There is something good about passing a newsstand and seeing the stacks of *World Almanacs* and *Information Please Almanacs* with the proud numbers of the new year on their covers. It's the first visual confirmation that the present year is concluding and a new one is to start, and the world is still here, and the country is still here and you are still here. Even almanacs are still here.

But with the coming of 1970 there was more than new almanacs to celebrate man's artificial marker of time spent because, of course, it wasn't just the year that was over. The decade was over and *Life* Magizine printed a double issue on all ten years, Harry Reasoner made an analysis of them, and Lawrence Welk devoted an hour to their finale, and all of that was as it should have been for, without it, no American could truly have felt the decade was done.

But in all the analyses, in all the retrospectives, in all the gathering of data there was an unusual kind of pride in simply the passing of time, almost a little arrogance, a recognition that we were witnesses to something quite extraordinary, a kind of conceit just to have lived through it and that we were alive "then."

Some said it was because it was the most exceptional time with the most exceptional men and the most exceptional events. But we all recognized that there were other exceptional times and other exceptional men and other exceptional events.

But there *was* something different about it.

It was not that we lived through it, but that we lived *in* it, were immersed in it, that was the difference: everyone was a part of every important moment, a part of every memorable event. It was the first *public* decade in the history of man.

How many people saw the bombardment of Fort Sumter in 1861?

But in the 1960s we not only read that men were fighting in a distant place. We stood by them and brushed through the scrub of jungle and heard the shots of war.

How many people stood at Kitty Hawk in 1903?

But in the 1960s we not only read of Man's new exploration. We watched the familiar faces of Shepard and Glenn and White and Armstrong—more familiar than some of our relatives—and we stood on the moon and saw ourselves 240,000 miles away.

How many people attended the funerals of President Lincoln or President Wilson or President Roosevelt?

But in the 1960s the funeral of President Kennedy was held in every American's home. His assassin was shot in millions of living rooms.

In the 1960s it seemed we were everywhere and saw everything. In its second decade, television became discontented with it's first decade's protegees of "Playhouse 90," "Studio One," "See it Now," "Person to Person," "Philco Theater," "Omnibus," "I Love Lucy," "Dragnet." It became discontented with its first decade's repertoire of tap dancers, Ed Sullivan, jugglers, Milton Berle and "Let Me Go, Lover," it became discontented with "Douglas Edwards and the News" and John Cameron Swayze's "Camel Caravan."

Television was suddenly on the minds and lips of everyone: Marshall McLuhan, Theodore White, the Vice President of the United States, the organizers of demonstrations, the Queen of England, and Tiny Tim.

Never before had any medium held the world so spellbound by its power, though the medium was still in its adolescence.

But it was death that invaded its adolescence and made it seem mature. As celebrities and lesser knowns and many warriors passed from earth, death became a frequent visitor to every home. Pictures of a horse that once amazed an audience, because the horse's hooves seemed to rise and fall on a scratchy piece of celluloid, were replaced by horses that pulled the caissons of Kennedy, Churchill, and Eisenhower through the homes of the nation. Those closest to Dr. Martin Luther King, Jr. and Senator Robert Kennedy and Senator Everett Dirksen were grief-stricken before millions of Americans.

Through television, the new generation was continually experiencing what past generations had largely been spared until much later in life.

In 1942, before the age of television, Carole Lombard was killed in an airplane accident. Half a year later, her last motion picture, Ernst Lubitsch's "To Be Or Not To Be," was released in theaters throughout the country. Many didn't see the film because they felt it was too soon to release a picture showing someone who so recently had died. That feeling was in no way unusual— for those days.

But with the acceptance of television, it became common to view living images of those who had passed away within months, within days, within hours, and even within minutes. It also became common to watch the living pass through the barrier of time. A famous actor would be 60 years old at 8 o'clock on Channel Two and 30 years old at 11 o'clock on Channel Thirteen.

History also was playing strange games with mortality. Seventeen years had passed without the death of a President or a former President. Then, within less than a decade would come the passing of Presidents Kennedy, Hoover, Eisenhower, Truman, and Johnson. Television would follow every moment of the processions.

Children became witnesses to life and aging and death in new time zones and it created a young-generation-in-a-hurry. Television imbued that generation with a feeling of urgency toward life. But there was no turning back. Some time after World War II, the American family had adopted and cared for an unplanned addition to their family called a television set, from which they expected and were granted unusual things.

By 1960 there were some 45,435,000 American families. There have been countless studies to determine what constitutes a typical American family, all of which have arrived at the conclusion that there is no typical American family. So, in fairness, to inspect the influence of their adoptee, we must focus on only one American family of the 1960s that was different from others but that did, at least, have much in common with many American families of the time. They were the Baileys of Frances Street in Aspen, Colorado.

Mr. Bailey was a ski instructor at a tourist lodge, Mrs. Bailey worked hard at home every day, their oldest child was ten-year old Susan, their second child was 21-inch Philco, and their youngest child was six-year old Leonard. It was a fine family.

Someone within the family was always getting sick, and so it was not at all alarming that ten-year old Susan had a temperature one Monday night in February. The Baileys didn't call a doctor that Monday night. They waited until Tuesday morning. There was, however, a different reaction to any disease that afflicted 21-inch Philco. On a Saturday night in March horizontal bars kept passing over Channel 9 of Philco. Those horizontal bars wouldn't stop. The Baileys had summoned someone for a house call within an hour.

While Philco was being treated, husband and wife sat watching the care he was recieving, with hope that he wouldn't have to go away for surgery but that he could be treated and cured at home. No matter the cost, it was worth it.

"He must be well—tonight."

Like watching a tennis match, they alternated their stares, first at Philco's tube, then at the strange man with the black grip, then back and forth again. Suddenly the tube went black. They clutched the arms of their chairs. It went light again. Then the miracle occured. The image was perfect without any moving horizontal bars. Mr. and Mrs. Bailey were exuberant. He put his hand on hers.

It was $72 for the house call and the medicine, and it was worth it. The color on the tube looked a little different after the strange and wonderful man left, but that would probably change back to normal in a short time.

Mr. and Mrs. Bailey hardly remembered life without Philco, or at least how life was spent without its predecessor, which was smaller and only black-and-white. (It was still alive, but had been moved into the bedroom, where it was happier with less duties in its twilight years.) They didn't know what effect television had had on them and on their family, but they suspected that its only real effect had been to provide something for the family to do—a means of entertainment and information. But it had been much more than something for them to do. And it had been much more than a means of entertainment and information.

The sordid reality was that a piece of furniture had become a member of the family.

As a member of that family, Philco was deeply trusted. The trust was not deserved. Philco was really no more than a transmitter of material recorded by a far-off camera—and the camera, in addition to all its more recognized capabilities, has one vice that goes unmentioned in the instruction manuals:

The camera is a liar.

All those lenses, viewfinders, turrets, cranks, and buttons have been made to preserve the visible on film or tape or to relay it for live transmission. It has been assumed that the visible is the truth. It's not. The *invisible* is the greatest truth.

Everything that is truly important is invisible. Peace is invisible. Freedom is invisible. Love is invisible. Faith is invisible. Even the motivation behind political decisions is largely invisible.

The camera says they aren't there.

The camera's inherent capacity to lie is compounded by the fact that when it *does* tell the truth, it does so with a deep, inborn prejudice, without which the camera would not know how to function. The prejudice it harbors is an antagonism against anything that is visually dull. It simply ignores the visually dull as though it did not exist and, instead, records the visually interesting. Since the visually dull is generally the more vital hint of the invisible truth, the camera successfully covers up its lies.

The cameras of news photographers are the most prejudiced of all. In the 1960s they showed the world America's slums without showing America's new housing developments for the poor. But they were being built. They showed the world America's police surging against a crowd without showing police risking their lives for the innocent. But they risked their lives for the innocent every day. They showed the world American students engaged in violence and disorder without showing them in classrooms. But they were there.

A riot? News.

No riot? That's not news.

A murder? News.

A life continuing from Monday to Tuesday? No news.

A baby found in Appalachia with a distended stomach? News.

Millions of well-fed babies? No news. No story. Not interesting. Not visual. Dull. Boring.

It is not visually interesting to watch a free border, to watch cars going across an unmarked line. Automobiles that go from New Hampshire to Vermont, from Nebraska to Iowa, or even from Michigan to Canada are dull and boring.

Peace is simply a yawn.

War isn't.

When cameras were put in choice positions around An Loc during a battle, the film was watched. If the same cameras had been put around Ann Arbor to watch the peace, there would have been no viewers.

Night after night all those little segments of film were building up into a grand visual entitled, "The United States of America and its Policies," and it had its effect. The camera stood guilty of having educated people in half-truths and non-truths. The six o'clock and six-thirty and seven o'clock news were not filmed records of the day's events; they were the filmed record of the day's abnormalities.

21

A new voyeuristic stigma affected the nation in those years. The more abnormal the image, the more it was watched. That stigma seemed to be a fad, like crowding into a phone booth or panty-raiding or making a hula hoop turn in uneven circles or streaking. But unlike a fad, it had a strange, sadistic, and inhumane element that seemed to breed on itself and demand still more abnormalities. The networks became the pushers that profited from the addiction that they had fostered.

In the 1960s, because of the immediacy of television network news, Americans were becoming news-oriented. But there is a great deal of difference between news orientation and fact orientation. Many say we now have more information than any generation before us. But news by itself can be misleading if not put in context with facts that are not news.

Near the end of that first public decade President Nixon used the term, "a silent majority." More regrettable than their silence was their invisibility and the prejudice that was exercised against them by the ever-increasing population of cameras. The invisible American rarely saw the lens of a camera aimed at him. Young people, old people, hard-working people, good people would die unrecorded on a permanent public medium because they were neither astronauts nor aberrationists, neither heroes nor hijackers, neither movie stars nor murderers.

The first generation with the capacity to make permanent the image and voice of man at any time of his life passed most of them by because they were too average and too normal, and there were just too many of them.

Occasionally, but only occasionally, the truth of abnormality worked in America's visual favor during the 1960s. Apollo was one of those rarities. It was a godsend because it obeyed the law of the lens.

Without the camera, 1969's Apollo Eleven would have been reduced to astronauts and NASA spokesmen speaking on radio and in lecture halls and in text. The proof that it had happened at all would have been a touring exhibition of moon rocks. But television was there, and Apollo Eleven was witnessed by millions. It was witnessed because Apollo Eleven was abnormal and its television coverage was extensive. As moon launches became more and more normal, their television coverage became less and less extensive.

Apollo was not the only abnormality to become normal.

There was Vietnam.

And as the conflict went on and on, its television coverage became more and more extensive. Someone was changing the rules on this subject because it was a negative one.

Vietnam *without* television might well have created a different psychological climate at home just as World War II might have seemed different *with* television.

At the beginning of U.S. involvement in World War II, the United States was not winning. The country mobilized, it backed its President, it fought and ended the totalitarian expansionism that it set out to annihilate. Had we not entered the war, there can be little question today that Europe would be a continent of masters and slaves with few, if any, minority groups surviving. Asia, too, would have come under a totalitarian regime. With or without Pearl Harbor and the German declaration of war on the United States, there would be little dissent today that our involvement was morally correct.

Add television.

Every night.

P-47s and P38s and B-17s and B-24s and B-29s.

Bombs.

Innocent victims.

Americans in Normandy.

Americans on Bataan.

Americans everywhere.

To learn of the progress of America and the Allies, Americans at home would not have heard the comforting voice of President Roosevelt on radio and they would not have imagined him sitting by a fireside. They would, instead, have seen him sitting in the Oval Office between two flags, until visually he would have become a bore. In addition, with Americans at home being witnesses to so much killing and bombing by Americans overseas every night on television, the President would have felt compelled to explain, to defend and to justify what the American military had to do. In short, instead of projecting confidence, he would have been forced onto the defensive.

Although Americans would have seen other Americans kill and bomb nightly, they would not have seen each night on television the killing of Jews and the interiors of concentration camps and the swarming masses of Nazi invaders. International photographers were not with the other side. In time, Americans at home might not have believed President Roosevelt, since their eyes would have been telling them other things.

When his speeches were over, his words would have been analyzed by people whom Americans knew better than they knew the President, because they would have seen them in their homes Monday through Friday.

If such was the case and if, indeed, Americans had watched the bombing and the victims of Hamburg and Berlin and Tokyo every night

23

without visual balance, it seems quite probable that World War II would not have ended in 1945, and perhaps we would not have won the conflict.

It is entirely possible that we can no longer fight wars in a visual age.

As South Vietnam faced defeat in April of 1975, Walter Cronkite of CBS was asked if he thought television could have changed the course of the war in Indochina if it had reported the war differently. He answered:

> Well, if it had not reported the war, perhaps. If it had failed to do its job, it might have had an effect on the war in Indochina. The fact that the American people saw the horror of war, night after night, lived the frustration of our policy in Vietnam through visual representation of what was happening out there, night after night, must have had an effect. I don't see how it could have failed to. This was what upset the administrations of both Lyndon Johnson and Richard Nixon so much was that the public was let in on the secret of what war is really like and what we were doing out there. It was impossible for them to carry on a foreign military policy behind the curtain of remoteness which wars of the past permitted.

Walter Cronkite, then, believed such televising was a forward step for the world, but he failed to note that Americans were given a false picture of the war since the opposing side was not witnessed on television. He also failed to consider what the citizens of North Vietnam had been viewing.

What Walter Cronkite perceived as being positive could, in reality, spell a world catastrophe.

It would surely be a great advance for civilization if wars were made untenable for all nations by the new visual age. That simply is not true. The thesis applies only to free societies of the world. Closed societies do not permit our form of television news programming and reporting, which means that in future conflicts closed societies may be able to fight —and win—without adequate resistance.

Ironically, the visual moving images shown during the Vietnam conflict that influenced the residents of Washington, Chicago, and Los Angeles were one and the same as the moving visual images that influenced the residents of Hanoi, Vinh, and Tanh Hoa in North Vietnam.

Neither the American nor the North Vietnamese audience watched a North Vietnamese "senator" indict the North Vietnamese "Secretary of State" or "Secretary of Defense." Both audiences watched U.S. Senator Fulbright indict our Secretary of State and our Secretary of Defense. Neither audience watched dissenters in North Vietnam. Both audiences watched films of United States dissidents.

24

While we watched critical commentaries following an address by President Johnson or President Nixon or President Ford, the North Vietnamese did not have analyses by critical commentators follow the speeches of Ho Chi Minh or Pham Van Dong or Ton Duc Thang.

Most importantly, scenes of war for all the audiences of the world were the scenes that sympathized with the North Vietnamese.

The United States Information Agency tried to correct part of that inequality between an open and closed society. A U.S.I.A. camera team was sent to Vietnam for two months with the mission of photographing visual proof of Viet Cong and North Vietnamese aggression. They failed.

The U.S.I.A. cinematographers could arrive only after the fact. Villages were attacked daily by the Viet Cong and the North Vietnamese, but neither the Viet Cong nor the North Vietnamese told the U.S.I.A. photographers where those attacks would occur. When the cameramen arrived, the gruesome evidence was there but the attackers were not, and so the evidence was not persuasive.

The Viet Cong and the North Vietnamese did not invite or wait for any international photographers. Americans and the South Vietnamese were escorted by them.

The U.S.I.A. discovered that the only three effective visual subjects obtainable regarding communist powers were:

1. Armed intervention that could be photographed as it occured, such as the Czechoslovakian invasion of 1968.
2. The Berlin Wall or other border areas that could be photographed from the west.
3. The flow of refugees into a free country.

The rest were either unphotographic or "after-the-event".

In the case of South Vietnam, without malicious intent by international photographers, but with questionable decision-making of New York producers, directors, editors, writers, and commentators, it appeared to the home audiences that weapons of war were in only American and South Vietnamese hands.

One particular night in the chronology of the conflict is now all but forgotten, and its television impact will surely go unrecorded in history books. It was November 3, 1969, which was a turning point in the history of both the Vietnam War and television news.

On that night two American networks chose to run different news clips of a brutal act of violence committed by South Vietnamese soldiers against an attacker from the Viet Cong. It was the same night the President appeared on television asking the country for unified support of American policy in the Vietnam conflict. The contrast between the two blocks of television fare was startling and took its toll.

In a visual sense, the President's speech was nothing more than one man talking to the camera, mostly in a chest-up shot, with those two flags, one placed to either side of him. Radio or print would have given the speech more impact, but not the same audience. Anyone who looked away from the President on television that night looked away because the scene was too little for the eyes. In contrast, the South Vietnamese brutality segment of the networks could not have had real impact on radio or in print. It would have gone almost unnoticed. Anyone who looked away from the news segment of brutality on television that night looked away because the scene was too much for the eyes.

That night, television visually worked against our involvement in Vietnam for a series of reasons:

1. The limitations of not being able to show the aggression of the other side.
2. The free access of cameramen to our own military and to the armed forces of our allies.
3. The willingness of networks to run such a film without balanced commentary.
4. The timing of such a film release.
5. The lack of visual impact within a Presidential address.
6. The inherent interest and boredom toward one piece of visual fare versus another within a short span of time.

Throughout the period of our involvement, the visual bias multiplied. Even in terms of dissent vs. support, the dissent was visible in masses protesting and demonstrating, whereas support was invisbile. Everything seemed to be working against our policy in a new visual age.

There was one final visual factor of television that is beyond calculation: engineers and technicians were in the process of learning their new crafts. They faced consoles with buttons, each one waiting to be pushed to bring instant images upon the television sets of the nation. The keyboards that plugged in the one-sided Vietnam news films were punched every night without thought of their total and collective impact, particularly when mixed with other television fare that made up the network news presentations.

Each night for all those years, American families watched the lush green jungles and saw Americans with guns and were given a death score. In the next instant they saw Jane Withers in a plumber's outfit

26

happily extrolling the virtues of a can of New Super Stain-Removing Comet. In the next instant they saw American abnormality at a university. The next night Vietnam death was bracketed between Feminique Deodorant Spray and the march of militants.

Our minds were accustomed to day and night in long stretches separated by dawn and dusk. The buttons pushed by technicians with inhumane rapidity in far-off control rooms created a pattern similiar to going outside and seeing day and night in one-, two-, and three-minute segments, one after the other. How could the human mind react to such a cadence of the unconnected?

Not well.

To press the right button at the right time is an awesome responsibility. If the astronauts aboard an Apollo mission had selected the wrong button at the wrong time, their capsule would have burned to oblivion. If a President had selected the wrong button at the wrong time, countries could have been destroyed. If television communicators selected the wrong button at the wrong time, human minds could have been influenced without logical basis.

Television images can mean life and death to someone. In a larger sense, those images can mean life and death to nations. Those images can be more powerful than a thousand armies—because armies can scorch only the skin, but television can scorch the mind.

In the 1960s many American families were scorched by their adopted piece of furniture, and for years forward they continued to be scorched by that extra member of the family.

The Baileys of Aspen, Colorado sat together at the end of the decade. Mr. Bailey didn't say much about what happened at the lodge. Mrs. Bailey didn't say much about what she did at home. Neither ten-year-old Susan nor six-year-old Leonard said much about what they learned in school. They all preferred to sit and watch Philco.

Philco loved to talk, and besides he showed pictures.

They had no idea that within a family room they were living in the Pearl Harbor of communications, with more bombs yet to come.

December the 7th, for this generation, was not a Sunday morning. It was the collective influence of the numbers on a channel selector and the deeply trusted pictures on a bright and colorful tube. Just as others had been told by someone in generations past, they too had been told by someone that seeing is believing.

Liar.

3

The
Shooting
Script

A strange thing happened with the demise of Tarzan and the loss of hats with bananas on them. As the fantasy images of Johnny Weissmuller, Carmen Miranda, Xavier Cugat, Sabu, Dennis Morgan, and Keye Luke faded out, new images of drama were fading in.

Africa became the scene of varied stories of struggling independence, national development, and apartheid. Latin America became the picture of proud nations, economic frustrations, and political turmoil. India was a population explosion, the Congress Party, and the question of Kashmir. The Mid-East was fragile borders, the eyepatch of Dyan, and the speeches of Nasser. And the Orient was the 38th parallel, the 17th parallel, and the monosyllabic television history of Ho, Mao, Ky, and Thieu.

Tan Son Nhut Air Base became more familiar to most Americans than O'Hare Airport. The Delta was more often a reference to the Mekong than to the Mississippi. The long bent shape on the map behind Cronkite and Reynolds and Smith and Huntley and Brinkley became more familiar than the shape of the coterminous 48 states.

The Vietnam War and television were both growing taller and getting pimples at the same time. Each was allergic to the other, but at the same time they were clinging to one another, sharing the experience of aging.

Visually, our involvement in the war was a dead duck. The only hope

29

was that those who were reporting and analyzing the war—both those in the national press and the national network reporters and journalists—would endeavor to put those visuals in perspective and would try to inform the nation of television's inherent weaknesses in covering a war.

Just the opposite.

From 1963 (when CBS and NBC expanded their network newscasts from 15 minutes to half an hour) through 1967 (when ABC followed suit), there was a total absence of narrative perspective. Their obligation and responsibility to their audiences were not met.

After 1968 began, television newscasting went one step downward: with the exception of Howard K. Smith, the television reporters and analysts added their own audible prejudices to enhance the prejudice of the cameras' visuals. It was as though they had become influenced by the images that came across their monitors, though they knew the inequities of those visuals.

The new-found narrative bias was the final blow to a conflict in which the backing of the citizens of the United States could mean the difference between freedom or defeat for the inhabitants of South Vietnam.

In 1968, Americans were being told by national television communicators that, if President Johnson would only stop the bombing, the North Vietnamese would negotiate a peace. (Eric Sevareid told his audience that we were ". . . one of the world's mightiest powers, bombing and smashing one of the weakest. . . .")

President Johnson stopped the bombing, and the communists only intensified their attacks.

The commentators' prophecy of communist response was wrong, but they went on to make further predictions while President Johnson was battered over and over again by the arms of national communications.

In 1970, when President Nixon ordered American troops into Cambodia to break up the North Vietnamese sanctuaries of supply, the communicators told the nation that it was an immoral invasion and that the United States would not get out of Cambodia once it had entered. President Nixon ignored their voices. The U.S. forces were out in the time limit he had specified, with most of the sanctuaries destroyed.

On May 6 of that year, CBS interviewed troops of Alpha Company who were about to embark off to the fighting in Cambodia. A CBS correspondent asked them four questions:

"What are you going to do?"

"Do you realize what can happen to you?"

"Are you scared?"

"Do you say the morale is pretty low in Alpha Company?"

The questions prompted Senator Robert Dole of Kansas to ask,"Does freedom of the press include the right to incite mutiny? . . .I believe a CBS reporter has come perilously close to attempting to incite mutiny by playing on the emotions of soldiers just before they were to go into battle. . . . I can think of no other war in our history where this sort of thing would have been permitted."

When the South Vietnamese went into Laos to break the Ho Chi Minh trail, we were again given the analysis of an immoral invasion, and again we were told the troops would never leave. The analysis was, once again, inaccurate.

When President Nixon made the decision to mine the ports of entry to North Vietnam, Americans were told by television commentators that it was reckless, that it would only lengthen America's military involvement in the war, and that it would destroy the scheduled summit meeting.

It shortened America's military involvement in the war, and the summit meeting was held on schedule.

At that time, however, a national commentator stayed above the crowd. He gave no rash, impulsive prediction of disaster, nor did he try to sway his viewers. Instead, he capsulized and reviewed the most important aspects of the President's address. John Chancellor told the news.

For this he was soundly reprimanded by what is often called the Bible of the industry, *Weekly Variety*. Reporting the news without bias frequently resulted in pressures upon newsmen by their peers to criticize the Administration. *Weekly Variety* stated:

> Plainly and simply, all down the line, CBS News has outclassed NBC, has been bolder, more courageous and more journalistically independent and responsible. The view is not a private one, but is shared by many of the Washington press corps, better able than most to compare because the two network newscasts play back to back in the capital. In pro circles, CBS is cited for a higher degree of professionalism and for a greater willingness to challenge Officialdom. It's also recognized by them, through the trials of CBS vice chairman Frank Stanton, that CBS News has corporate backing . . . .
>
> The night President Nixon appropriated prime-time to announce the mining of Haiphong harbor as a new stage in the Vietnam War, the NBC "instant analysis" was little more than a recap of the speech with some electronic razzle-dazzle that brought in audio from correspondents in Hong Kong and Moscow speculating on the implications at the Communist powers and surmising that it would doom the Moscow summit.
>
> In contrast, CBS pundits were definitely committal in words as well as in gesture (Eric Sevareid shaking his head and saying, "I see no end to this").

31

Days after the President's new military action, on May 9, CBS was on the air in prime time with a comprehensive examination and no-nonsense analysis of that development in the special report, "Escalation In Vietnam: Reasons, Risks and Reactions." Nothing comparable from NBC.

John Chancellor did the unexpected and did not conform to false analysis—and was condemned by *Weekly Variety*. Some others did the expected and tried through inaccurate assessments to sway the American public against the Adminstration's policy—and they were complimented by *Weekly Variety*.

Shortly after the President made that request for national unity regarding the mining of ports of entry to North Vietnam, CBS Evening News chose to exhibit a North Vietnamese propaganda film of American prisoners of war in Hanoi expressing themselves against that decision of the President and against the policy of the United States.

It is worth noting that the greatest difficulty in the visual medium is not getting the right script, or budget, or cast, or technicians, or equipment. The greatest difficulty is in getting a meaningful distribution. The North Vietnamese had a willing and ready-made distribution apparatus that reached 16 million Americans in one night at the time they wanted to reach them. Walter Cronkite's CBS Evening News was the single most important ally to Hanoi's propaganda distribution circuit: the North Vietnamese produced a propaganda film for primary release to American citizens, designed to be viewed at a time when *they* wanted American citizens to rally against the President's actions, and CBS provided the means of exhibition on schedule.

Paradoxically, films made by the United States Government that gave a viewpoint in opposition to Hanoi were not allowed to be exhibited to U.S. audiences.

Frank Shakespeare, who led the United States Information Agency from 1969 through 1972, was one of the few creative people in the nation who was telling the true story of Vietnam through publications, radio, exhibits, motion pictures, and television. His unparalleled leadership of the Agency drew many creative talents to his side. John Ford, perhaps the greatest filmmaker of all time, made his last motion picture "Vietnam! Vietnam!" for Shakespeare's U.S.I.A. But, in most cases, (including "Vietnam! Vietnam!) a Congressional resolution prohibited the domestic exhibition of films of the United States Information Agency. While Senator Fulbright was attempting to initiate even tighter restrictive legislation, distraught because of a New York television exhibition of the U.S.I.A. film on the Soviet invasion of Czechoslovakia, he was simultaneously demanding that the State Department grant visas to four Cuban filmmakers so they could stage a Cuban Propaganda Film Festival in New York.

Through 1970, 1971, and 1972, with domestic competition nil, the visual bias of network news increased, the narrative bias likewise accelerated, with the loudest television outcry occurring in December of 1972, when President Nixon ordered the bombing of Hanoi and Haiphong.

Walter Cronkite (CBS) said "Soviet News Agency Tass said hundreds of U.S. bombers had destroyed thousands of homes, most of them in the Hanoi-Haiphong area" . . ."And Hanoi Radio said the bombings indicate President Nixon has taken leave of his senses." Walter Cronkite left it at that.

Dan Rather (CBS) said the United States "has embarked on a large-scale terror bombing" with the operative word,"unrestricted." He quoted Hanoi to the effect that the strikes were "extermination raids on many populous areas."

Eric Sevareid (CBS) said, (with sources known only to himself) "In most areas of this government . . . the feeling is one of dismay, tinged with shame that the United States is again resorting to mass killing in an effort to end the killing."

Harry Reasoner (ABC) said, " . . . Dr. Kissinger's boss had broken Dr. Kissinger's word. It's very hard to swallow . . . Backing off from a cease-fire is a weight and comes very close to a breaking of faith, with Hanoi maybe, with Americans most certainly."

Simultaneously, the print medium confirmed the instant television analysis: James Reston wrote, "This is war by tantrum and it's worse than the Cambodian and Laotian invasions."

Anthony Lewis wrote, "Even with sympathy for the men who fly American planes, and for their families, one has to recognize the greater courage of the North Vietnamese people . . . the elected leader of the greatest democracy acts like a maddened tyrant . . . To send B52's against populous areas such as Hanoi or Haiphong can have only one purpose: terror. It was the response of a man so overwhelmed by his sense of inadequacy and frustration that he had to strike out, punish, destroy."

The New York Times wrote that waves of bombers "flying in wedges of three, lay down more than 65 tons of bombs at a time, in a carpet pattern one and one-half miles long and one mile wide . . . the most intensive aerial bombardment in history . . . equivalent to twenty of the atomic bombs dropped on Hiroshima." The *Times* informed its readers that all of this was occurring in "densely populated areas." (Four months later and after American military involvement in Vietnam was over, *The New York Times* reported "Hanoi Films Show No Carpet Bombing." Late, but at least corrected.)

Joseph Kraft wrote, " . . . Mr. Nixon called on the bombers—an action, in my judgement, of senseless terror which stains the good name of America."

A *Washington Post* editorial said, "He has conducted a bombing policy . . . so ruthless and so difficult to fathom politically, as to cause millions of Americans to cringe in shame and to wonder at their President's very sanity."

Only months before the prisioners of war arrived back home, CBS presented a travelogue of North Vietnam narrated by John Hart of CBS, who reported from Hanoi:

> There is frequent laughter . . . Yesterday when I suggested that we'd like to get up early some morning to film the sunrise over one of these lakes, it was suggested that's a wonderful idea because after all, the American flyers cannot bomb the sun . . . Within a few hours [of my arrival] I have seen a richness in hospitality and a richness in hope . . . Five-thirty Sunday morning in Hanoi: This is the second Mass of the day. The cathedral is filled . . . [American peace workers] will be taken to see destroyed buildings and towns, and especially a number of destroyed or partially destroyed churches . . . There is a display of forgiveness by the villagers [toward captured pilots] . . . being released under the humanitarian policy of the government.

As Americans watched his films, a painting was shown and the painting was described as "recalling a bay . . . lovely . . . before it was heavily bombed." There were films of hospitals and churches bombed and damaged by Americans. There were no films of factories or bridges or railroads or supply centers bombed. No war objectives of any sort were shown .

John Hart of CBS continued the travelogue with interviews of captured American prisioners of war, and through John Hart and through CBS their statements went into the homes of Americans, just as Hanoi wanted: "I have been well treated since my capture and I would like to thank the people for their kindness . . . their humanity has also been shown by their release of three prisoners recently . . . I hope my government may soon bring this war to an end . . . To my family, my lovely wife, I would wish that they select the candidate they feel will stop this war."

President Nixon ignored the American exhibition of Hanoi propaganda and American television analysis, and as a direct result of his bombing policy the North Vietnamese and Viet Cong agreed to negotiate with the

United States and South Vietnam in Paris. The South Vietnamese agreed to the signing of the Paris Peace Accords with U.S. assurances that, if the communists broke the cease-fire, America would respond with "vigorous reactions" and, in accordance with the Paris agreements, would resupply South Vietnam with military equipment on a one-for-one ratio to cover their losses. American military involvement in Vietnam was over within one month after the inception of the December-January bombing.

It was not, as in other times, that America had been engaged primarily in a military war. Instead, from the President through the foot soldier, those Americans engaged in the defense of the South Vietnamese were fighting two wars simultaneously. One was a war against the aggressors in Asia, the other was a war to reject the constant bombardment of biased reporting and analysis.

A study of the Institute for American Strategy has demonstrated that, during 1972 and 1973, CBS News balance between favorable and unfavorable stories regarding U.S. military affairs was: 13% favorable, 66.1% unfavorable. The study found that in 1972 83.33% of themes in CBS stories about South Vietnam were critical of the Saigon government, while 57.32% about North Vietnam were favorable to Hanoi. Within the same year the study found that CBS quoted the statements of those who were critical of our policy 842 times, while those in favor of our policy were quoted 23 times.

The stark proof of the impact and influence of years of biased reporting presented itself in early 1973 when our former prisoners of war disembarked from their rescue aircraft at Clark Air Force Base in the Philippines. There was genuine shock in America, not only from those who opposed, but also from those who supported our Vietnam policy, when former prisioners of war came off the aircraft holding American flags and waving banners reading,"God Bless America" and "God Bless President Nixon" and coming to microphones to tell of their long-held support of U.S. policy, their belief that President Nixon's decision to bomb North Vietnam had been the only acceptable course, and that those Americans in North Vietnam's prisons applauded and cheered when they heard the bombs. There was equal shock to hear of the atrocities the North Vietnamese had committed against their prisoners.

Why were so many in our nation shocked?

Because of the visuals we had seen for so many years.

Because of the narrative we had heard for so many years.

Because we had become victims of the display of one-sided news reporting.

Because of the analyses.

Because of the unanalyzed exhibition of North Vietnamese propaganda films showing American prisoners of war speaking against our policies and against our leaders and telling us that they were well treated by their Communist captors.

As a result of the comments made by the former prisoners of war when they arrived at Clark Air Force Base, some went so far as to speculate that the former prisoners were brainwashed on the plane that took them from Hanoi to the Philippines.

But *they* were not brainwashed. Perhaps others were. In 1935, Edward Banse, in his book entitled *Germany Prepares for War,* wrote:

> It is essential to attack the enemy nation's weak spots—and what nation has not its weak spots? You must undermine, crush, break down its resistance and convince it that it is being deceived, misled and brought to destruction by its own government. This is done to cause it to lose confidence in the justice of its cause so that the opposition at home . . . may raise its head and make trouble more successfully than ever before. The original well knit, solid, powerful fabric of the enemy nation must be gradually disintegrated, broken down, rotted, so that it falls to pieces like a fungus when one treads on it in the woods.

On January 24, 1973 our invitation to a ten-year war via television and the press was to begin a two-year intermission.

During the 1960s and the early 1970s, we as a nation spent a large share of our lives, of our power, of our prestige, and of our treasure for the freedom of another people in another country on another continent. We lived and many died through our most moral and responsible decade in terms of national unselfishness.

We also lived and many died through the most immoral and irresponsible decade that had yet occurred in terms of our domestic communications.

The national communicators had to redeem themselves.

Watergate.

4

Background Music

Could it have happened to any other President?

There wasn't an experienced politician in Washington during 1973 and 1974 who didn't know that the rules of many generations of political life were being changed in the middle of the game: the rules by which all experienced politicians in Washington during 1973 and 1974 either had themselves played or had hidden lest the revelation expose others who were their friends. The middle of the game was called the Nixon Administration.

It was surely the tapes that provided the final bullets in an ironic suicide, but the President had already been mortally wounded by the sudden changing of rules that had resulted from the creation of a climate. Before those final bullets, the House Committee on the Judiciary had already adopted three articles of impeachment arrived at through the inequity of a year and a half of climate creation.

If "all the President's men" from another administration had been subjects of nonstop investigative reporting, if they were publicly interrogated, if all their files were opened, if their memos were read on national television, if their logs were examined, if Congressional committees were established, if a special prosecutor was appointed, all while the most important national communicators worked toward the President's removal from office, what President would have been immune from a public disaster? None.

To open any administration's logs and records and diaries and thought processes would, of course, have raised immediate questions. President Nixon's predecessor, Lyndon B. Johnson, can serve as an example, not because he was corrupt—he was not—but because he was immune. Powerful Democrats, unlike powerful Republicans, have been immunized from scrutiny by virtue of their numbers within the Congress and by virtue of their numbers within the federal bureaucracy and by virtue of their numbers within the media. And so there was no senator or GS-15 or television commentator on the Evening News during President Johnson's administration who would raise the following questions:

Was there a vote fraud in Texas in his first election to the Senate and again in 1960 when he was the Vice Presidential candidate?

Who ordered the bugging of Senator Goldwater in 1964?

What was the connection between the President and Billy Sol Estes?

Why did the President order electronic surveillance of Dr. Martin Luther King and other civil rights leaders in 1964?

Did the President try to cover up the Walter Jenkins case?

Were government funds used to enhance the President's property in Johnson City?

Were the records of government payments in Johnson City destroyed?

Did the taxpayers finance the President's personal airstrip?

Was it for national security or was it for political reasons that the President ordered the FBI to find out if five government officials were "close to Robert Kennedy"?

Why did the President have the FBI bug Spiro Agnew's airplane in 1968?

How did the President become a millionaire after being born in poverty and following a lifelong career as a public servant?

What was the connection between the President and the riches of Bobby Baker?

President Johnson wrote, "Bobby Baker could have ruined me." But Bobby Baker did not ruin President Johnson. When the Senate held a roll call vote on whether to investigate Bobby Baker or not, among those voting against such an investigation were Senators Ervin, Talmadge, Inouye, and Montoya, who were later to become all the Democratic members of the Senate Select Committee investigating the campaign practices of 1972. Most commentators in the national media gave the Johnson-Baker connection scant attention, and virtually no investigative reporting was directed toward it.

It is all too obvious that, if President Johnson had had the same coalition of critics that belabored President Nixon, the questions already asked would have multiplied and multiplied again, as would be true with any President. Service in the public life breeds a record of public and private conduct that, in turn, can always breed a list of charges where the will of the opposition exists.

As was true of President Johnson, President John Kennedy was also immune from such opposition. Ben Bradlee, editor of *The Washington Post,* admits that "the press generally protected Kennedy as it protected all candidates from excesses of language, and his blunt, often disparaging characterizations of other politicians." It was a half year after the resignation of President Nixon that Ben Bradlee admitted he had been privy to an extraordinary piece of conversation fourteen-and-a-half years prior to his revelation:

> Over dinner, he [President Kennedy] told how he had called Chicago's mayor, Richard Daley, while Illinois was hanging in the balance to ask how he was doing. "Mr. President," Kennedy quoted Daley as saying, "with a little bit of luck and help of a few close friends, you're going to carry Illinois." Later, when Nixon was being urged to contest the 1960 election, I often wondered about that statement.

Thus for fourteen and a half years Ben Bradlee of *The Washington Post* was involved in a cover-up of valuable information relating to the possible theft of an American election. He heard the conversation, he "often wondered about that statement", yet did nothing—not even any investigative reporting assigned within his own publication.

Ben Bradlee's admission was not big news. Many had thought that the election was stolen in Cooke County, Illinois, and parts of Texas. As Bradlee suggested, Richard Nixon was being urged at the time to challenge the election's results. Nixon decided not to make such a challenge as he felt it would have severely damaged the American Presidency. Surely, the thievery of an election is the ultimate in American political criminality, but the national media virtually ignored the possibility. Beyond the fact that *The Washington Post* passed over investigative reporting, there were no damaging commentaries on television, and within the federal government there were no investigatory committees formed and no special prosecutor appointed. None of the above occurred even after Bradlee's long-delayed admission. The "truth-seeking" national media with "America's right to know" as their first priority were, in this case, smiling and winking in the hallways.

39

With so much damaging information known about other administrations, why the media uproar over "Watergate"?

Why President Nixon?

1. He was, simply, Nixon. Hardly a charismatic figure by the standards of national analysts. He was not one of their "good guys".
2. He had been criticized by many politically liberally oriented members of the press since his first Congressional race in California against Jerry Voorhis. The criticism became a loathing throughout the investigation of Alger Hiss, and the loathing reached a peak as he defeated Helen Gahagan Douglas for senator in California. It continued throughout his Vice-Presidency and exploded in the California gubernatorial campaign of 1962.
3. He was the first President during their mature lifetimes who was a Republican with the stated proclamation that he leaned toward conservatism. Politically and philosophically, he was abhorrent to their own beliefs.
4. His policies regarding Southeast Asia, which they condemned, ended our military involvement and brought home our men who were prisoners of war. At that time the commentators did not know that the America of 1975 would not keep America's word of 1973, and at that time it appeared as though South Vietnam had a reasonable chance to remain free.

It has been argued that the most powerful national communicators—CBS, NBC, ABC, *Time* magazine, *Newsweek* magazine, *The New York Times,* and *The Washington Post*—did not hold a liberal bias and that a liberal bias was and remains no more than a Nixonian fantasy. Many members of those national news organizations have argued that they take an adversary role toward every administration, and that their adversary role is in the nation's interest as it tends to reveal to the public all the strengths and weaknesses of every issue advocated by the administration in power. There is a good deal of theoretical logic behind that explanation of the role of the media vis-á-vis the Presidency. But unfortunately the most powerful national news organizations are adversaries only to the domestic and international policies that tend to lean to the conservative side of the political spectrum. The more liberal domestic and international policies of an administration are either ignored or more often advocated by the mistermed adversary relationship.

President Johnson was met by an adversary relationship from the most powerful news communicators, not for his liberal programs, but for his conservative policies. It was not the continuation of the New Frontier or his inception of the War on Poverty or his Great Society programs that activated the opposition of so many within the media. It was his defense appropriations and the Dominican Republic crisis and his policy regarding Vietnam.

During President Nixon's first term there was little if any criticism from those same forces of national communications regarding policies that were, in fact, opposed by many conservatives. The commentators did not take an adversary relationship to his trip to the People's Republic of China or his detente with the Soviet Union or his appropriation proposals for the arts and humanities or his wage and price controls or his proposed Family Assistance Plan. It was only his more conservative policies that drew their criticism: his Anti-Ballistic Missile Program, his Supreme Court nominations, his Vietnam policy, the Cambodian incursion.

As President Nixon entered his second term, his conservatism was all too obviously mirrored in a number of his policy pronouncements. There was the impoundment of funds, his strong no-amnesty stand, the New Federalism, his plans to cut and depoliticize the federal bureauracy, his accent on a strong military defense, his attempted dismantling of the Office of Economic Opportunity and other Great Society programs, and his speeches regarding the work ethic. The attacks from the national media came hot and heavy. He could not, however, be done away with for his policies of conservatism.

President Ford was greeted with enthusiam as the same news communicators became ecstatic with the destruction of the electorate's conservative decision of 1972, ecstatic with the rumored rise of liberals to appointed positions after they had been defeated by the voters, ecstatic with a proposal for amnesty for draft evaders and deserters.

In the face of such consistent subjectivity, the question must be asked: Can a news communicator be totally objective?

Probably not.

Nikita Khrushchev once told President Kennedy, "There are neutral nations, but there are no neutral men." His observation seems not only to be true, but to be substantiated by the admissions of newsmen.

David Brinkley said, "Anyone who is totally objective should be locked up."

Dan Rather compared objectivity to "the Ten Commandments, a goal worth reaching for but impossible to live up to."

Tom Brokaw said he couldn't go on with his "gut feelings based on personal biases" unless the feeling is "based on bits and pieces that add up to a little more fabric" and then he could "put the White House position into my own perspective . . . I never say flat out what I don't believe. If I really can't accept what the White House is telling me, you'll see some sign of that."

Walter Cronkite was asked if there was some truth in the view held that television newsmen tend to be left of center. He replied, "Well, certainly liberal and possibly left of center as well. I would have to accept that."

But it is the American people who should not accept that. Just like other politically astute citizens, those who communicate the news *do* have a political point of view. The *tragedy* is not that the media are *too* biased, but that they are not biased *enough* in broader areas of the political spectrum.

Those who argue that networks were equally balanced during those years cite Howard K. Smith as the counterweight conservative. Howard K. Smith did support U.S. policy within his commentaries on Vietnam, which was a welcome relief from the unanimity of the others but he, alone, could not provide a balance. Further, and more to the point of balance consistency, he described himself as a liberal and his commentaries on other subjects substantiated his assessment. The balance, then, was of one issue for a period of time from one half of a news team on one of three networks.

It is not that Brinkley and Rather and Brokaw and Cronkite and Sevaried and Mudd and Schorr and Reasoner and Wallace and Kalb and Pierpoint and Paxton and Reynolds and Stern and Morton and Safer and Perkins and Laurence and Peterson and Mackin and Graham and Herman and Snyder and Schieffer and Hart and Stahl and Collingwood and Schoumacher and Utley and all the others should have been replaced with those of a neutral view. "There are no neutral men," Khrushchev told Kennedy. There should, simply, have been a reasonable balance by use of those who had *another* view.

The liberal bias came into being simply because the creative arts attracted more people of a liberal persuasion than of a conservative outlook. Journalism and television are, of course, not simply methods of communication: they are creative arts. A liberal political view within large national news organizations was nothing more than an unavoidable infection that became contagious. But within CBS, NBC, ABC, *Time* magazine, *Newsweek* magazine, *The New York Times*, and *The Washington Post* it was allowed to become an unchecked epidemic.

The young newcomer to such national news organizations quickly found out what was acceptable and nonacceptable, what garnered him organizational compliments and what garnered him organizational complaints, what raised him in the eyes of his managers and co-workers and what diminished him in their eyes. If his political instincts were less than absolute upon his arrival, with few exceptions they became absolute in a short time.

In contrast with those national news organizations were many responsible news organizations that abhorred the liberal bias emanating from one or more of those mentioned. Although there were responsible national news organizations and hundreds of local news organizations, even their collective power was in no way commensurate with that of CBS, NBC, ABC, *Time, Newsweek, The New York Times* and *The Washington Post.*

Some outside of the media call the liberal bias of the major news organizations a conspiracy, but it is not. It is, instead, a political and philosophical "gentlemen's agreement". Each organization *knows* how it is *supposed* to think. Instincts are not conspiratorial, and it is instincts that have created the liberal bias.

When fast news judgments must be made and deadlines must be met, political instincts become as important as creative instincts. Without *diverse* political instincts taking part in the making of fast judgments, public climates that are difficult to discern as the days go on can be created. Climates have been created time and time again on issues large and small.

The period in our history inaccurately called "Watergate" is the textbook lesson of the creation of a climate.

Watergate is the complex of buildings in which occurred the break-in to Democratic National Headquarters on June 17, 1972. The same commentators who misguided home audiences through the American military involvement in the Vietnam conflict established the word "Watergate" as the umbrella over any and every accusation made against the adminstration. No matter if it was the President's taxes or the ITT case or the Vesco case or political contributions, it all became "Watergate".

But there was an immensely deceptive and destructive element in the use of that catch phrase for unrelated subjects. The break-in to the Watergate was a *known crime.* By labeling all other charges under the umbrella of "Watergate," they seemed to be linked to that known crime, and there was an implied guilt by association. This was not only done to unrelated incidents, but to people within the administration who had no relationship to that crime.

The technique for its accomplishment was simple. The television commentator would read a report while the screen behind his desk illustrated the Watergate complex of buildings. The implied result of the narrative simultaneous with the visual was that there was some association between the two. The backdrop of the Watergate complex became an all-pervading lethal tool as innocent names were paraded before it. The commentator was not guilty of *saying* something that was inaccurate

43

by the use of this technique, but a combined visual and audible statement was created, and it was untrue.

When the administration called attention to the unfairness in using "Watergate" as the broad catch-phrase for any and every charge leveled against it, the answer continually came back from those who used the technique that the word and image of "Watergate" were merely journalistic shorthand for the whole scope of charges, and that everyone understood their use of the word and image.

But long after the word caught on and endured, John Mitchell and Maurice Stans were acquitted of charges in the New York trial regarding campaign contributions linked with Robert Vesco. The same people within the media who advocated the shorthand of "Watergate" and who had used it earlier in reference to those political contributions, had a sudden compulsion to explain and be precise by telling their audiences upon acquittal that, "of course, this was *not* a Watergate case."

Suddenly the word was given a very precise definition, which in fact meant that the word was used when it could be destructive to the administration, but not when it could be helpful to the administration.

Under that umbrella, the box was opened, and those private papers and records and taxes and diaries were examined and analyzed on national television and in the press. It provided a familiar litany: break-in, dairy funds, ITT, use of executive agencies, San Clemente property financing, Key Biscayne property financing, the Vesco case, Cambodia bombing, impoundment of funds, the special investigative unit, dirty tricks, corporate campaign funds, and the President's gifts to his wife. Night after night, one charge followed another.

There were "so many things" leveled against the Nixon administration that if a defender answered one, another was charged until "so many things" became "too many things".

After a year and a half of publicized charges, the American Civil Liberties Union was able to devise a list of some 19 charges, and the staff of the House Committee on the Judiciary advocated 56 areas of inquiry, including such subjects as the dismantling of the O.E.O., allegations against the Environmental Protection Agency, charges against the Cost of Living Council, and claims against the Small Business Administration. The climate, once created, was maintained, and those who perpetuated it did not care for *what* charge the President was driven from office, as long as he was removed.

John Osborne of the *The New Republic* believed that the press performed a necessary and proper function in getting at the basic facts of the charges against the Nixon administration, "but," he added, "I have

44

to say at the same time that they're like dogs who have scented blood and running the fox right down to the death."

As the climate permeated Washington, and then the nation, many people concluded with sincere regret that the President should resign. Most in that category stated that their conclusion was not based on a reaction to any single incident or event, but on what they saw to be the cumulative effects of the entire list of charges.

"The list" technique was the continuing strategy of the news organizations ever since they made the word "Watergate" their phrase of encapsulation that gave all allegations a criminal implication. The technique of "the list" is as old as the history of propaganda. It has been used for causes both good and evil. Its most effective and tyrannical use was by Joseph Goebbels, who advanced the list technique in regard to the alleged offenses of Jews in Hitler's Germany. The result of the technique is that no one knows what the crime is, but there are "so many things" that, in confusion, they conclude that at least one or more of the charges must be true. To one degree or another, many political campaign managers have used the list technique to try to discredit an opponent.

In this case, with no hurry-up of a target date for an election, the list technique evolved drop by drop on national television and in the press.

Although none within the national media admitted to the importance of climate-creation, members of the House Judiciary Committee did.

One of the President's critics on the House Judiciary Committee, Representative Harold Froehlich of Wisconsin, confessed, "We went fishing. And we played every issue we could for whatever it was worth. Part of it was creating an atmosphere for impeachment."

Another of the President's critics on the committee, Representative Jerome Waldie of California stated that issues had been used to provide thunder and lightning—even if no rain: "I think all of these things make an ultimate pattern which influences this vote, even though a member cites another single issue. My guess is that it took this entire pattern of conduct to bring many members to a vote for impeachment . . . Certainly it provides a symphony in the background."

The symphony was being conducted by network television, playing to the national audience for a year and a half. Its orchestration and performance were masterful. Its composer remained anonymous to most of the millions who watched as the musicians played their instruments almost flawlessly.

5

Lights,
Action,
Camera

Television commentators and members of the press simply ask too much of American Presidents. They not only want them to behave as gods, but they ask more of them than they ask of the gods. I am not so sure they would let a President get away with smashing the stones on which God had written the Ten Commandments. Moses did. I am not sure they would let a President get away with creating a disturbance in a market place. Jesus did. I am not so sure they would let a President get away with abandoning his wife and children to meditate. Buddha did. They don't even let a President get away with perspiring. Nixon didn't.

When the President smiled, the East Room was silent.

When he wiped the perspiration above his upper lip with the side of his index finger, the East Room seemed to shake from an eruption of noise as Nikons and Canons clicked and snapped and motor drives whirred between exposures with more fast clicking and snapping and whirring to capture as many pictures as possible before his hand came back down to his side. Public harassment of the President by the media had become the national sport, and the East Room had become the site of the new Super Bowl. The players were rising from the bench as soon as he paused, anxious to get into the game. Their national image was at stake. To be disrespectful or rude could increase their prestige among their peers, as well as increase their recognition factor in the nation's living rooms.

Hugh Sidey of *Time* magazine commented on the conduct of the White House Press Corps conducting a Presidential press conference: "dreadful performance . . . questions scornful and impolite . . . bear pit . . . two hundred reporters leaping up and screaming for attention . . . absolute impoliteness, unnecessary rudeness . . ."

It was at one such press conference on October 26, 1973 that the President, when asked about the media, said he had never heard or seen such outrageous, vicious, distorted reporting in 27 years of public life. The reporters looked at each other with alarm. They didn't know why he would say a thing like that.

Could he have been offended by the things they were writing in the press and saying on television? Could he have been so sensitive as to have been offended by a syndicated column that was published that very day in *The Washington Star-News* headlined, "Has President Nixon Gone Crazy?" Carl Rowan's compassionate pen wrote:

> . . . Those who wonder about the President's emotional balance have now begun to suspect that even in the face of a vote to impeach he might try as "commander-in-chief" to use the military forces to keep himself in power. If that sounds far-fetched, consider the aftermath of Richardson's refusal [with a laudable display of courage and honor] to fire Cox. Nixon's new chief of staff, General Alexander M. Haig, Jr., ordered Ruckelshaus to fire Cox. When Ruckelshaus, with impeccable integrity, refused to do so, Haig said: "Your commander-in-chief has given you an order." Haig might just as easily have said: "The Fuehrer has spoken."

Interesting parallel.

Other parallels were to follow. But outrageous, vicious, and distorted? There was, for example, Nicholas von Hoffman's parallel on CBS' "Sixty Minutes" of July 28, 1974:

> . . . What we're debating now is how to dispose of the body. The President is like a dead mouse on the American family kitchen floor. The question is, who is going to pick it up by the tail and drop it in the trash? At this point it makes no big difference whether he resigns, thereby depositing himself in a sanitary container, or whether Congress scoops him up in the dustpan of impeachment. But, as an urgent national health measure, we've got to get that decomposing political corpse out of the White House. Interment should be short and quick. Send no flowers, please.

It was not, however, the editorials that were the most harmful to the President. Their point of view was too obvious. The greater harm was done by the sophisticated and subtle use of news reporting, cloaked as

48

always to appear impartial and accurate and without bias. Although no single example might be seen as being outrageous and vicious, there were so many distortions that there was a collective outrageousness and viciousness as each distortion was heaped upon another. Like funds in a savings and loan institution, the interest was compounded daily, and its year-end net was staggering.

As television network news was cited more and more as a medium of bias, many within the nation recognized that network news did *seem* biased, but they often shared a how-do-you-put-your-finger-on-it frustration. That frustration was occasioned by techniques of the trade that, when used, indeed biased the news, but left the network's disguise of innocence intact and unwrinkled.

Thomas Collins of *Newsday* commented: " . . . A television man will cross over between straight reporting and analyzing and interpreting to a point that even sophisticated viewers would be hard pressed to say where one left off and the other began. The result, from a print man's point of view, is a dazzling disregard for hundred-year-old formulas."

In examination of the television techniques used, it must be remembered that news does not simply occur and is then simply reported on television. Events occur. Someone decides if a particular event is worth reporting. Someone decides how it should be reported. Someone decides what the narrative should be. Someone decides how the narrative should be read. Someone decides what moving visuals or graphics should be used. There is a whole slate of decisions to be made. Within those decisions, the techniques employed can influence the audience's receptivity to a particular event. These techniques are the "fine print" of television that pass by virtually unnoticed and unchallenged. Some are used by instinct. Some are used by design.

It took centuries for the literate population to understand the techniques employed through various uses of the printed word, to understand that the fine print was often more important than the bold print, to understand that a phrase could imply one thing while saying another.

Since we don't have centuries to spare, it is time to itemize some of the fine print in use by the newest and most influential mass medium of communication. It is time to list some of those techniques that can discredit ideas and people and can also be used to advance other ideas and other people.

The following is an alphabet of visual and audio television news techniques, with an example provided of prior utilization. In the case of some techniques that call for more than one example, and particularly those of frequent use, several examples are given.

A. <u>STORY PLACEMENT</u>:   The first story on a network newscast is largely perceived by the audience as being the most important news of the
day; the second story, the second most important news of the day; and so
on through the first group of stories.

If a network would like to give particular significance to a story or less
significance to a story, their placement within the newscast establishes an
immediate priority of importance within the viewer's mind.

Examples: 1. During the 1973-74 period, the prime placement of so-
called "Watergate" stories, even when such news was minimal, became a
common and ongoing technique to increase audience interest in the
charges against the administration.

2. On January 18, 1974, a peace agreement was signed between Israel
and Egypt in the Sinai Desert. It was, in fact, the first official meeting
between Israelis and Egyptians since Moses said to the Pharaoh, "Let my
people go." The Sinai peace-signing was relegated to Story No. 5 on the
CBS Evening News, appearing after (a) Richard Ben-Veniste, (b) Wilbur
Mills talking about President Nixon's taxes, (c) Tip O'Neill, and (d) Edward Morgan and the latest Uher 5000 and Dictabelt development.

3. The day the Arab oil embargo of 1974 was lifted, which was a story
directly and immediately affecting everyone in the United States, that
story was relegated to follow the "Watergate" news on CBS.

B. <u>THE HOLD FRAME</u>:   This is an old motion picture technique,
which now has wider use in television than in theatrical films. Since
November 1963 it has been often referred to as the "Jack Ruby Frame."
(When Ruby killed Lee Harvey Oswald, the technique was used on re-
plays of the video tape to visually stop the action at the moment the
bullet hit Oswald.) The technique is used to "catch" something the audience might otherwise have missed. It interrupts the motion to hold on
one still picture from the moving action so that a particular frozen image
can be examined by the viewer. In sporting events such as football or the
finish line of a close horse race, the hold frame is particularly useful.

It can also be used to give the *impression* of "catching" an event it did
not "catch" or "catching" a person it did not "catch." In late 1972, CBS
reviewed charges against members of the White House Staff. CBS
showed pictures of two working associates of President Nixon and implied, not with words but with visuals, that those two men were guilty of
"something."

Close–shot footage and portraits of the men were available, but close–
shot footage or portraits would not have served the visual intent. CBS
chose to run a long shot of the two walking together in raincoats and

then, at a precise moment when their faces were exposed to the camera CBS used the "Jack Ruby Frame" to freeze the action. It looked as though CBS had "caught them at something." CBS knew the audience was subconsciously accustomed to this technique to catch something they would have normally missed. One could have filmed Eric Sevareid and Walter Cronkite together and frozen the action, showing both of their faces to make the point. "See? We caught them." But caught them doing what?

C. SELECTIVE SEGMENTATION: What was once a primitive or at least sloppy technique has become what is almost impossible to distinguish as it comes across the screen. The network's objective is to cut out portions of a speaker's comment and, by use of tied-together excerpts in false continuity, make the total effect different from his original in-context remarks. The primitive method was simply to physically cut out the film of the undesired area and splice the two remaining wanted ends together. This results in a jump-cut, which can be seen by the audience and leaves room for suspicion and looks crude. The professional device is to use a cut-a-way of an interviewer or a cut-a-way of someone's reaction to the speaker or a cut-a-way of a chart, or whatever seems appropriate, and then cut back to the speaker. Both the visual and audio cut can be accomplished while the cut-a-way is on screen. This can be used, and is most often used quite ethically to excerpt, cut down, or give certain segments of a speaker's performance without jarring visual effects, as would be evident without a cut-a-way. But it can and has been used unethically to change the emphasis and meaning of what someone has said.

Example: CBS' much awarded, Emmy-winning, "The Selling of the Pentagon" (1971) is the most blatant example of the unethical use of this technique. CBS went so far as to use portions of an answer to one question as an answer to another question, with the accomplished intent of making Daniel Henkin, Assistant Secretary of Defense for Public Affairs, look foolish.

It is difficult to recognize an excerption. At times, but not always, it can be ascertained by an inconsistency in audio quality behind the cut-a-way or as the shot changes.

D.   COMMENTATOR SPECULATIONS THAT APPEAR TO BE FAC-TUAL: Although the words are couched and the periods are in the right places separating information from speculation, the end effect of this technique is to give the listener the impression that only facts are being reported. The transient character of television airways reporting permits this to be effective whereas, if the report were printed in a newspaper or magazine for examination, there would be risk of discovery.

Example: Daniel Schorr wrapped up his October 18, 1974 report on the CIA by stating, "The era of covert operations isn't ending, just evolving. There's reason to believe that right now in there, they're working on contingency plans, if called upon, for some of the world's unstable areas. Portugal, Spain, Italy, the Arab Oil States could be the next target."

"There's reason to believe" couched one sentence of speculation. The last sentence was totally worthless and couched with the words "could be" but, because of the specificity of nations and regions named, the audience impression was that Daniel Schorr was telling facts.

E. THE TRUTH BUT NOT THE WHOLE TRUTH: Although the whole truth is known to the reporter or commentator, only a portion is told, which casts an invalid impression by intent.

Examples: 1. Dan Rather reported a story that had appeared in *The Wall Street Journal* that alleged President Nixon had "soundly slapped" a man in Orlando, Florida. Rather stressed the fine professional reputation of the reporter who wrote the story. Dan Rather did not report the follow-up story that also had appeared in the *The Wall Street Journal* the day before Rather's newscast in which the man who purportedly had been slapped stated: "I wasn't slapped. I was affectionately tapped on the cheek. It's the greatest thing that ever happened to me."

2. On March 25, 1974 the NBC "Today" Show had a report that Senator Howard Baker of Tennessee had stated on the previous day's "Face the Nation" (CBS) that President Nixon should be more forthcoming and give the Judiciary Committee whatever tapes and documents they required. Senator Baker had balanced his suggestion on "Face the Nation" by saying that the Judiciary Committee should also be more forthcoming by allowing James St. Clair to cross-examine witnesses appearing before the committee. The "Today" Show audience gathered that Senator Baker was critical only of the President and not that he was equally critical of the committee.

3. Senator Barry Goldwater's criticism of President Nixon was given wide network coverage, but when Senator Goldwater also accused the press of being "hounds of destruction," his statement was given no network news coverage.

4. When Senator James Buckley called for the resignation of President Nixon, the networks reported his statement in depth with one omission.

None of the networks included the Senator's attack within that same statement on what he called the media's reckless exploitation of Watergate or Senator Buckley's concern of aiding media and other critics in subverting the 1972 mandate.

5. In early 1974 wide network attention was given to all special elections and primary elections in which either Republicans or Nixon supporters lost. When General William Westmoreland lost the Republican gubernatorial primary election in South Carolina the results of the election were given similar wide network attention, but there was no mention on any network that the winner of the primary, James B. Edwards, was a staunch Nixon supporter, whereas Westmoreland had taken a neutral position toward the President.

6. When the President visited Huntsville, Alabama on February 18, 1974 Tom Brokaw of NBC News commented that thousands of federal workers in Huntsville were given the day off to greet the President. It was true that the federal workers of Huntsville were given the day off, but NBC failed to say that it was the national observance of George Washington's birthday and federal workers throughout the United States were given the day off as they had always been in observance of that holiday. (Ken Clawson, Director of Communications of the White House, telephoned Tom Brokaw that evening and asked that the item be corrected. Tom Brokaw admitted the error but there was no retraction on NBC until three months later, on May 31, 1974, after the NBC error was cited by a White House spokesman and reported by the wire services.)

7. In CBS' "Castro, Cuba and the U.S.A." televised on October 22, 1974, Dan Rather sought to convey the impression that Castro had abandoned revolutions in other Latin American countries and had changed to talk "more of conciliation and trade." Rather said,"Che [Guevara] went to Bolivia in 1967, was killed there trying to carry out a Castro-style war. Che's way failed. Now, Castro talks more of conciliation and trade. Indeed, while keeping Che's memory alive in Cuba, Castro is pushing elsewhere an economic union of all Latin American nations."

As Accuracy in Media, Inc. pointed out (of course, to be ignored), CBS was privy to the original filmed interview between Frank Mankiewicz and Kirby Jones with Fidel Castro, parts of which were used in the televised "Castro, Cuba and the U.S.A." Within that interview, but not used in the televised production, Castro said: "Do we sympathize with revolutionaries? Yes, we do. Have we aided revolutionaries as much as we have been able to? Yes, we have." Castro was asked under what conditions he would support other revolutionaries and answered, "It is essential that they be fighting. If they are not, then we don't. When they do fight, we back them." What Castro was saying was a complete contradiction of the point Rather made. CBS did not include those conflicting remarks of Castro within its telecast.

F. CATCH PHRASES: With unnoticed and unattributed bias, an editorialized catch-phrase is added to the nation's vocabulary, by force of habit. Catch phrasing is a printed-word and audio technique that has been streamlined by television with the use of "Anti-War Movement," "Peace Movement," "The Saturday Night Massacre," "The Mysterious Alert," "Operation Candor," "The White House Germans," and "The Christmas Bombing" (and, as previously mentioned, the word "Watergate" itself, used to house all charges of the period). The streamlining was applied by using catch phrases as matter-of-fact routine and by repetition as "fact phrases," making them appear to be nonbiased actualities.

Examples: 1. The terms "Anti-War" and "Peace Movement" suggested that those who opposed the movement were "Pro-War" and/or "Anti-Peace." The "Anti-War" and "Peace Movement" was, in actuality, the Anti-U.S. Policy Movement and, for the sake of accuracy, it should have been referred to in that manner. As the years progressed, it became more and more apparent that some within the movement were opposed not only to U.S. policy, but advocated the victory of the North Vietnamese, the Viet Cong, and the Khmer Rouge, though they were never referred to as Pro-Communist, but only as "Anti-War" and "Peace" advocates.

2. "The Saturday Night Massacre" became the phrase used for the discharge of Archibald Cox and the resignations of Elliott Richardson and William Ruckelshaus. "Massacre" conjures images of murder in the old West or the murders of St. Valentine's day. "The Monday Night Massacre" was *not* used for the April 30, 1973 White House termination of Bob Haldeman, John Ehrlichman and John Dean. That night was not selected for stigmatization, since the national media were pleased to see them go.

There was an awkward, repeated attempt to label President Ford's pardon of President Nixon as "The Sunday Morning Massacre," but it met with no success.

3. "The Mysterious Alert" was used as the title and the theme of a CBS documentary referring to the Mid-East Crisis of 1973. At the time, many who opposed President Nixon were suggesting that he called the alert to divert the nation's attention from the charges being made against him.

Although CBS admitted within its documentary that intelligence had been received that 50,000 Soviet paratroopers had been placed on combat-ready status, that reports had been received that a Soviet airborne troop headquarters had been activated in Southern Russia, that Soviet troop carriers had been reported flying toward Egypt, and that a brutally frank note had been sent to President Nixon from Chairman Brezhnev in which he threatened unilateral action in the Israel-Arab conflict, CBS continued the theme and title of "The Mysterious Alert," continuing the suggestion that President Nixon and Secretary Kissinger might have created a national alert for domestic political purposes.

4. Network news repetition of the *Newsweek*-invented phrase "Operation Candor" meant that, unless the President continually remained on the defensive, his opposition within the media could announce that "Operation Candor" was over, with the conclusion that candor itself was merely a passing phase. They did exactly that.

5. Bob Haldeman and John Ehrlichman were often referred to by the media as "The White House Germans" (even as late as March 31, 1975, almost two years after they left the White House: Mike Wallace, CBS). Would it have been acceptable to call Stanley Scott or John Calhoon "The White House Blacks" or Leonard Garment and Dr. Kissinger "The White House Jews"? Of course not. But "The White House Germans" was a prejudicial slur against the administration that the media felt was palatable.

6. "The Christmas Bombing" was the catch phrase used to identify the decision of President Nixon to bomb Hanoi and Haiphong. I suppose this was done since both Christmas and the bombing occurred in December. The bombing could have been called "The December Bombing to Bring About the January Release of the Prisoners of War." It wasn't.

The bombing actually started on December 18 and was suspended for 36 hours for Christmas and 36 hours for New Year's. Inaccuracy was used to achieve a purpose.

G. UTILIZING THE CHEMISTRY OF COMBINED AUDIO AND VISUAL: Often a visual image gives one impression, the audio gives another, and the combination of the two used simultaneously creates a distortion. (Most significantly, as mentioned, this technique was used to inject "Watergate," without the use of word, by the projection of the Watergate complex on the rear screen behind the commentator while he talked of an unrelated story.) The modifications of this technique are endless.

Examples: 1. At the time when some were speculating that President

55

Nixon made his 1974 trip to the Mid-East to direct attention away from the charges made against him, ABC gave a report regarding those charges while behind the commentator the word "Watergate" appeared on the screen. The commentator went on to give a report on the President's Mid-East trip, and the words "Mid-East Trip" appeared without the removal of the word "Watergate," which was now placed directly above the new phrase. As the commentator gave his report on the trip, the visual: "Watergate Mid-East Trip" was staring at the television audience.

2. CBS Evening News of June 26, 1974 started with the story of President Nixon arriving in Brussels at NATO Headquarters. Dan Rather began the report, "The President looked tired and sleepy as he arrived at NATO Headquarters just outside of Brussels, but he smiled a lot, made jokes and seemed to become more alert and enthusiastic as the morning went along." Later within the newscast of that story Rather stated: "Eager to shake hands, the President a few times reached out where there were no hands to shake or where the hands he sought were not so eager." In neither case did the visuals justify the narrative, but it *appeared* as though they did, as the viewer's eyes quickly sought to find any sign for confirmation of Rather's words. The positive impact of the visuals, had they been presented without editorialized narrative, was lost.

H. VISUAL EMPHASIS OF AUDIO BY SELECTION OF PHRASES FOR THE AUDIENCE TO READ: Charles Guggenheim effectively used this technique of printed words upon the screen in the television commercials for Senator McGovern's race for the Presidency.

Examples: 1. The technique was steadily applied by the networks as a method to emphasize out-of-context areas of the transcripts of President Nixon's tape recordings.

2. In CBS' "Castro, Cuba and the U.S.A.," televised on October 22, 1974, which highlighted an interview with Fidel Castro conducted by Dan Rather and Frank Mankiewicz, the printed word technique was used to underscore particular statements of Castro as the interview commenced. The phrases selected for the technique created a meaningful collective impression. Phrases chosen were:

"We see Ford with a certain hope."

"I do not believe that Kissinger is hostile toward Cuba."

"You have found a correct formula to liquidate the Nixon matter."

"Nixon proposed the armed forces of the United States be used. Kennedy had taken a courageous stand."

"Guantanamo is a piece of the national territory of Cuba."
"In the United States, capitalism has given the maximum results."
"The Soviets are absolutely loyal in their relations toward Cuba."
"They [United States] owned the Cuban economy."
"I knew Allende well."
"The revolution has succeeded."
"Women do a great deal of work."
A totally different impression could have been given by a choice of other phrases such as, "To create a revolution, I believe force is needed and a force of arms is needed."

I. PRETENSE BALANCING: The motive is to show that the presentation is showing all sides of a particular story when, in fact, the balance is tilted.

Examples: 1. On Vietnam Veteran's Day of 1974, there were three segments to CBS' news coverage of that event. The first segment was the ceremony at Arlington National Cemetery, the second was a story of Vietnam veterans who were demonstrating on Capitol Hill, and the third was the story of a veteran whose face had been blown to bits in the Vietnam conflict and who had terrible and unjust problems with the Veteran's Administration. This left the audience with three stories "regarding Vietnam Veteran's Day," one favorable and two unfavorable. The favorable story and the first unfavorable story (the dissenters on Capitol Hill) were truly news stories of activities performed in recognition of Vietnam Veteran's Day. The third story, which tilted the balance, was not a news story, but a story that had been reported months previously on the network news.

2. On July 22, 1974 CBS telecast James St. Clair's briefing to the press. Bruce Morton's wrap-up after the briefing ended with : "One last comment: Mr. St. Clair is an advocate. The viewer should keep that in mind. He is a skillful advocate; a skillful lawyer. And, like any good lawyer, he argues his client's side of the case: one side of the case." This sudden concern with identification of a lawyer's point of view was not the case when it came to Samuel Dash, Richard Ben-Veniste, Terry Lenzner, Jillwine Volmer, Ruthus Edmiston, John Doar, or any other adversary of the President.

3. When a network endorses or opposes a candidate, always without admission, utilization is made of pretense balancing within "news" stories pertaining to the election. For the 1975 Philadelphia mayoralty Democratic primary between incumbent Frank Rizzo and Louis Hill, pretense balancing was used by CBS as both candidates were shown,

57

along with the issues. As is frequently the case in national coverage of a local election, some of the report was used to give the background of each candidate, since the national audience might not have been familiar with those backgrounds:

> *Regarding Rizzo's Background:* Frank L. Rizzo, Democratic Mayor of Philadelphia since 1971, when the former police commissioner campaigned and won as the toughest cop in America. In the four years since, Democrat Rizzo has, among other things, strongly endorsed Republican Richard Nixon, withheld from the Democratic organization that first backed him all of the extensive patronage at his disposal, supported a slate of Republican losers in the 1973 local election, formed a special police unit that was later revealed to be investigating his Democratic enemies, and finally, lost out in a lie detector contest with the Democratic City Chairman, who had charged Rizzo with attempted bribery. An expert said Rizzo lied. The Mayor still denies it.
>
> *Regarding Hill's Background:* Rizzo's primary opponent is State Senator Lou Hill, former Marine, a lawyer, and a legislator generally acknowledged to have been outstanding over the past nine years, but also generally acknowledged to have a campaign style that ranges from bland to blah.

J. SELECTIVITY OF INTERVIEWEES: The meaning of a news event can be given a decided tilt by those selected to be interviewed.

Examples: 1. On the Monday following Archibald Cox's discharge, the networks ran 19 Congressional attacks on President Nixon and two defenses, though this was not a representative sampling of the Congress.

2. Within days of Cox's discharge, Walter Cronkite gave Archibald Cox 11 minutes of network *news* time in a single interview, without any defender of the President. It was the longest single interview ever given on a nightly network news presentation. Prior to the Cox interview, the only other two special interviews Cronkite had conducted on the CBS Evening News were with John Dean and Daniel Ellsberg.

K. TREATMENT AND RESPECT GIVEN AN INTERVIEWEE: The audience is immediately given an impression about the person being interviewed by the questions he is asked and by the manner in which he is addressed by the reporter conducting the interview.

Examples: 1. The difference in both the context of the questions and the manner in which they were put by Dan Rather to President Nixon in comparison with Dan Rather to Fidel Castro provides the most revealing illustration. It proved that an interviewer can be an adversary or a straight man at his own discretion.

2. Shortly after the announcement of President Ford's amnesty plan, Dan Schorr of CBS interviewed a draft evader with a display of courtesy one would think would have been reserved for Pope Paul VI. Although Schorr had asked questions of those in the Nixon administration as though he were volleying cannon balls, his questions to the draft evader were delivered with the tap and impact of a beach ball. Using the license reserved only for journalists, Schorr participated in the cover-up of the name and face of the evader as well as the locale in which he was hiding. The obvious questions, such as asking what the evader thought of those who served or those who were wounded or those who were killed or those who were jailed because they didn't hide, were not asked.

Neither Schorr nor any other nationally televised interviewer chose to interview any returned prisoner of war to ask their opinions of the amnesty proposals.

L. PROMPTING AN INTERVIEWEE: Words can easily be put into an interviewee's mouth by the interviewer. It is most effective if the interviewer's question is phrased so that it can be cut out, while the answer is retained as a complete statement. Obviously, if the manner in which the interviewee answers is not a complete statement, the question cannot be omitted. The objective is to coach the interviewee.

Example: On November 11, 1974 there was a report on the NBC Nightly News concerning the acquittal of the National Guardsmen who were involved in the Kent State tragedies of 1970. The prosecuting attorney being interviewed by the reporter seemed to accept the judge's decision of acquittal and, in the spirit of accepting a trial's resolution, he was not expressing any bitterness. In desperation, the NBC reporter asked, "Do you feel the unanswered questions will ever be answered? There are a lot of unanswered questions." That brought about the response he wanted, even though the reporter had to offer his own view.

M. METHODS OF READING: Reading slow or reading fast or an accent on a particular word or a faint smile or a shake of the head give editorialization that cannot be found by rereading the text of the report or interview, but can be found only by viewing and listening to the newscast.

Example: The Mike Wallace interviews of Bob Haldeman (March 24 and 31, 1975) were the most blatant editorials given in this manner, with the incredulous stare, the pulling back of the head in suprise, the sudden changes of tone in voice, and sarcastic smiles.

N. Visual Authority: Every executive knows that a desk can give a visual sense of importance to the man who sits behind it. When in the company of a visitor, most executives follow the rule of rising from the chair behind the desk and walking to another chair without the separation of the desk as a barrier of importance between host and guest. The very visual posture of a commentator gives him a look of authority.

Example: All network newscasts. In contrast, within most cities of the United States, television viewers feel a kinship with their local weatherman. He's "one of them," or at least it certainly appears that way. He is generally the only interior performer in the local evening news shows who is standing. He's on their terms. The easy informality of Willian F. Buckley, Jr. on "Firing Line" and of David Susskind on "Open End" sans desks puts them on even levels with their guests and with their audiences.

O. Narration Rather Than Visuals—When It Suits The Purpose: Often a news event will occur in which visuals will create a negative effect when the producer hopes to achieve a positive impression, or a positive effect when the network hopes to achieve a negative impression. In this case, visuals defeat the purpose, and only narrative is used.

Example: When President Nixon worked in his Executive Office Building Suite, Dan Rather would refer to it as "his small, hideaway office" to CBS viewers. There were stills available of the office, but stills would have defeated the purpose of Dan Rather's line, since the office was a very large one, used as his working quarters. The term "hideaway" was also inaccurate. Dan Rather was informed when the President went to work within his Executive Office Building suite, as were all the members of the White House Press Corps. It was, in fact, a more public suite than the Oval Office as it was the one place the public could see him enter and exit as they watched from the street. Dan Rather's continual referral to it as "the President's small, hideaway office" had a sinister ring of secrecy and isolation, and it could have raised suspicions in the minds of some viewers: "What is he doing there?" "Why does he go to a small hideaway?"

P. Re-Cap of Past News to Relate to Present: While telling a real news event, a re-cap is given to something that happened days, even weeks ago, as though it had a direct relation to the current event. In that way audience interest may be revived in a non-news story.

Examples: 1. Again, the entire period when charges were made against the Nixon Administration serves as the best running example.

2. The Vietnam Veteran's Day story, mentioned in *Technique I,* also applies as an example of the re-cap technique, which was used effectively in that case.

3. The networks frequently reminded their viewers during the discussion of impeachment that Gerald Ford had once said that an impeachable offense is "whatever a majority of the House of Representatives considers it to be at a given moment in history," in contradistinction to the administration view that an impeachable offense must be an indictable crime. Gerald Ford had made the statement during the Justice Douglas impeachment controversy of 1970. The networks failed to remind their audience that Gerald Ford was referring to a lifetime job of a Justice of the Supreme Court, whose tenure in office depends on "good behavior" and that Ford had also said within that 1970 debate (again, prior to the controversy of impeachment regarding President Nixon): "The President and Vice-President can be thrown out of office by the voters at least every four years. To remove them in mid-term . . . would indeed require crimes of the magnitude of treason and bribery."

Q. CREDITING AND DISCREDITING: This newswriting technique is designed to give credit to an editorial factor of the writer's choosing.

Examples: 1. On October 18, 1974 Senator Henry Jackson realized a victory with the announcement that emigration of Russian Jews would be less restrictive in the future. On December 18, 1974 Chairman Brezhnev denied the change in emigration policy. When it was a victory for Senator Jackson, Walter Cronkite said, ". . . it was the Democratic Senator who led the fight to ease the emigration restrictions . . ." When the policy failed, Senator Jackson's political party was not mentioned by CBS.

2. The National Citizens' Committee for Fairness to the Presidency was referred to both by NBC and CBS as "a group that calls itself The National Citizens' Committee for Fairness to the Presidency." "A group that calls itself" sounds as though it might not *really* be what its name implies. But the organization was truly national; with people representing every state of the Union, it was certainly a committee composed of citizens, and its purpose was surely to advocate fairness to the Presidency. Yet the term "a group that calls itself" was never prefixed by NBC or CBS to the American Civil Liberties Union or Common Cause or Americans for Democratic Action or, for that matter, the Symbionese Liberation Army, though it was hardly liberating anyone, was not an army, and had a membership of seven people. The name persisted even after its membership had declined to three (CBS, April 18, 1975). The group

61

was further distinguished by the networks and other within the national media by their reference to it as the S.L.A.

3. Prior to the time President Nixon visited the 8th Congressional District of Michigan, Jack Paxton of NBC gave a report of the feeling of residents within that district. He reported that, in the urban areas of Michigan's thumb district, the people were highly critical of the President (which most were in that area). He illustrated by quotes such as "He ought to be impeached" and "I hate him." He went on to say that "in rural areas, which are more conservative, the people are reluctant to criticize the President." The precise truth was that in the rural areas of the district, they strongly *supported* the President. Why not say that?

4. NBC reported that President Nixon's Mid-East Trip was taken "with the stated purpose of cementing relations [between the United States and the countries of the Mid-East]." The words "with the stated purpose" were an implication that perhaps the real purpose was not being stated. This was done at the time when some were saying that the President made the trip to distract attention from the charges against him.

5. NBC announced on January 11, 1975 that President Ford's amnesty program had failed because, in the network's opinion, not enough deserters and draft evaders were taking advantage of the offer. There was no comment made that success or failure was not dependent upon who did not take advantage of the program, but rather that the offer, itself, was the objective.

6. When President Nixon returned from his 1974 trip to the Mid-East he immediately held a meeting with Congressional leaders. Dan Rather of CBS commented that the President held the meeting "anxious to maintain the momentum of his Mid-East trip." The President held the meeting to advise the Congressional leadership of what had occurred on the trip. If he had chosen not to have had such a meeting there would have been wide and valid criticism, with Dan Rather likely saying the President did not meet with the Congressional leadership "anxious to maintain a distance from Congressional questions."

7. On the day Dwight Chapin pleaded innocent to all charges, David Schoumacher of ABC commented that Mr. Chapin was once the man to see if you wanted to visit the President and "if there was once a public Chapin" who handled the President's appointments, "there was also a secret Chapin who directed guerrilla war against the Democrats." ABC's conviction of a charge for which Dwight Chapin was not even indicted probably went unnoticed by many, but its subliminal effect was false, slanderous, and a violation of the presumption of innocence.

8. Although President Nixon had received great criticism for "isolation" and "seclusion" and for not getting out into the country, when the President made a trip to Jackson, Mississippi, CBS Morning News commented, "President Nixon has trouble finding friends in Washington, D.C., so he gets out when he can."

R. CREATION OF NEWS: Sometimes there is no event during the day relating to a continuing story that the network wants to sustain. Creating a related event is no real problem. One method is for the network to send a newsman and a camera crew over to the Capitol to talk to a senator or congressman about "the story." If the congressman or senator is willing, he or she can make news in an instant. Many are willing, since it is an opportunity to be seen and heard by millions. Networks generally recognize a particular senator's or congressman's point of view before an interview is filmed. If it doesn't turn out as they want, it can be discarded. Other methods of creating news are to give an unimportant item an extended story length, to have reporters quote other reporters, or to emphasize the fact that there is no news regarding a "continuing story."

Examples: 1. CBS Network News had three separate reports on Bebe Rebozo's Key Biscayne bank and a savings and loan application, with one of the reports running eight minutes in length. From the length and number of such reports the viewer was left with the impression that influence peddling was involved on a massive scale. CBS did not find any proof of any wrongdoing, as Robert Pierpoint of CBS himself admitted (on radio). The series of reports on a so-called *news* show helped to convict Bebe Rebozo in the public mind.

2. Following Dr. Kissinger's October 25, 1973 press conference regarding the Mideast alert, NBC Nightly News reran all four questions asked by members of the media of Dr. Kissinger, dealing with the charge that the President fomented the crisis relating to the Middle East for domestic political reasons.

It was reasonable that the newsmen asked the questions, but it was distortion and prejudicial for all four of the questions to be excerpted as an out-of-context impression of the press conference, which lasted over an hour. In this way a network, through *selected* replay of reporter's questions, was creating the news rather than giving a faithful overview of the briefing.

3. When President Nixon delivered a 1974 speech to the Daughters of the American Revolution, Walter Cronkite of CBS commented that not once in the speech did the President mention Watergate or impeachment or domestic crisis.

The President also did not mention Patty Hearst or the battle in the Golan Heights between Syria and Israel or the economy. The purpose of the speech was not intended to cover every interest. In short, even when there was no news on "Watergate" or impeachment, news was made of the fact that there was no news regarding those subjects in an effort to create ongoing interest. Dan Rather used the same line in a report on President Nixon's briefing to Congressional leaders regarding the Mid-East.

S. The Inclusion or Omission of Crowd Reaction: When reporting a speech of a public figure, it is up to the film editor to decide whether to include the audience reaction of those witnessing the speech. Most often, reaction will be cut in the interest of time, but this is an option that can change the entire character of the address. The character *can* be retained without the loss of time by leaving in the applause, fading it to a low level, and bringing in the reporter's voice above the applause. During an election campaign report showing two candidates, this technique of inclusion or omission can be used to tilt the character of public reaction to one candidate against another.

Example: During the 1974 election campaign, NBC's report on the New York Senate race between Jacob Javits and Ramsey Clark used this applause and reaction technique to the advantage of Ramsey Clark and to the detriment of Jacob Javits.

T. Focal Length: Different lenses give separate impressions of the size of a crowd. Every photographer or cinematographer knows that a large crowd can look small, and a small crowd can look large by simply changing from a long lens to a short one, which changes the focal length. Television viewers who want to know the size of a crowd should look for the margins of crowd-ends, as it is the only sure manner in which to make an accurate judgment.

Example: CBS coverage of President Nixon's trip to Jackson, Mississippi, on April 25, 1974, which visually minimized his supporters.

U. Tragedy and Comedy Reporting: There is no hiding of passions within this type of reporting. The commentator comes right out with it.

Examples: 1. John Chancellor, usually one of the most responsible commentators, gave a chilling example of dramatic tragedy reporting on the night of Archibald Cox's discharge and the resignations of Elliott Richardson and William Ruckelshaus. When televised passion exceeds

64

the immediate magnitude of the event, such excess can sometimes create its ultimate importance. The following are excerpts from John Chancellor's report:

> The country, tonight, is in the midst of what may be the most serious constitutional crisis in its history . . . That is a stunning development, and nothing even remotely like it has happened in all of our history . . . You are watching a special NBC Report of another event this year that we never believed would have happened in the history of this Republic . . . A constitutional situation that is without precedent in the history of this Republic . . . In my career as a correspondent, I never thought I would be announcing these things . . .

Obviously, dramatic reporting is human, understandable, and often valuable, as in the case of the death of a national figure or in the event of a natural disaster. But when it involves an element of political or partisan controversy, or both, it can be destructive.

2. When comedy is used irresponsibly, just as in the case of tragedy, it can have a devastating effect upon a political figure. When Governor Connolly was acquitted of all charges in the dairy fund case, he was asked by CBS reporter Lee Thornton if, following his indictment, trial, and subsequent acquittal, he could regain enough public confidence to participate in political life. Connolly answered that within our system of justice he should be able to involve himself in political life again and that after all of the probing he had undergone for 18 months, he probably had a badge of innocence. Rodger Mudd, as anchor-man ended the Lee Thornton Report in the following manner: "It's reminiscent of a quote attributed to Humphrey on election night, 1968. 'Whoopee,' he said, 'we lost.' "

V. Oblique Emphasis Reporting: This is the most important and most often used technique of network news. Seemingly straight reports are very often subtle editorializations. The use of words and phrases gives transient and subliminal points of view to the audience, most often without audience knowledge.

Example: On October 1, 1974, CBS reported the opening of the trial of Bob Haldeman, John Ehrlichman, John Mitchell, Robert Mardian, and Kenneth Parkinson. CBS' Fred Graham opened the report with:

> A central issue of the case is whether the passions and publicity of Watergate will prevent a fair trial, yet only a handful of protestors showed up as the once-powerful Nixon High Command came to court. Somebody

spat on John Ehrlichman's coat, but Kenneth Parkinson passed almost unnoticed. John Mitchell showed he still has enough clout to wheel in through the Judge's entrance, and H.R. Haldeman and Robert Mardian slipped through a back door into the courtroom.

An examination of that paragraph gives five illustrations of point-of-view reporting:

1. "A central issue of the case is whether the passions and publicity of Watergate will prevent a fair trial, *yet* only a handful of protestors showed up . . . " The word "yet" suggests a disqualification of the preceding phrase.

2. " . . . as the once powerful *Nixon High Command* came to court . . . " "High Command" is a military term, not the term used for Presidential appointees.

3. " . . . Somebody spat on John Ehrlichman's coat, *but* Kenneth Parkinson passed almost unnoticed . . ." The word "but," just as the word "yet," is a disqualifier, which in this case suggests that spitting on John Ehrlichman may only have been a fluke.

4. " . . . John Mitchell showed *he still has enough clout to wheel in* through the Judge's entrance . . ." It was not because of clout, but because none of the other defendants requested permission to park within the building.

5. " . . . and H.R. Haldeman and Robert Mardian *slipped through* a back door into the courtroom." Did they "slip through" the back door or did they "walk in"?

Let us assume that the reporter wanted to influence the audience in the opposite direction. He could have said:

A central issue of the case is whether the passions and publicity of the past two years will prevent a fair trial. Public knowledge of the case and deep-seated passions were evident by protestors who appeared early to view the defendants' arrival. One of the protestors spat upon John Ehrlichman's coat. Kenneth Parkinson, who is not as well known as the central figures, was able to avoid the hostility of the protestors by nonrecognition. John Mitchell drove into the underground parking garage to escape the mob, while H.R. Haldeman and Robert Mardian came into the courthouse through a back door for the same reason.

Straight news reporting would have been:

A central issue of the case is whether the passions and publicity of this case will prevent a fair trial. (Number of) protestors showed up to view the previous administration appointees come to court. John Ehrlichman and Kenneth Parkinson used the main entrance to the courthouse and someone who recognized Erhlichman spat on his coat. Kenneth Parkinson went unrecognized. John Mitchell drove into the building's parking garage, while H.R. Haldeman and Robert Mardian came into the courthouse through a back door.

W. IGNORING FOLLOW-UP STORIES: Follow-up stories are often ignored when their usage would be beneficial to those the networks oppose or harmful to those the networks endorse. This technique is similar to, but not quite the same as, a total disregard of an important story, to which we devote a later chapter.

Examples: 1. All networks reported the 1974 layoffs of TWA and United Air Lines employees, which was true and damaging to the administration. None of the networks reported the 1974 rehiring of those TWA and United Air Lines employees, which was true and helpful to the administration.

2. Howard Hunt testified before the Senate Select Committee about spy work that was conducted against Senator Barry Goldwater in 1964. The story died the next day.

3. In October 1974 the NBC and CBS networks carried a "source" report that Richard A. Moore, Special Counsel to the President, had been named as an additional unindicted coconspirator. *The New York Times* carried the same "source" story on the front page. The Special Prosecutor's office immediately issued a formal denial of the story. The next day, *The New York Times* mentioned the Special Prosecutor's correction on page 14. However, CBS and NBC never referred to the Prosecutor's denial in any way. Mr. Moore asked NBC reporter Carl Stern, who had broken the original incorrect story, whether NBC would at least mention the correction as the *Times* had done. Carl Stern replied, "I would like to, but as a television man you should know that's not the nature of the beast." Mr. Moore never was named a coconspirator, unindicted or otherwise, or even called as a witness, but the damaging story remains extant, staining in the public record a man otherwise known for the highest integrity. Indeed, journalist-politican Frank Mankiewicz, in his book *U.S. v Nixon,* published several months later, mentioned the report that Richard Moore had been named an unindicted coconspirator, but never mentions the fact that the report was officially proven false.

X. STORY ASSOCIATION AND GROUPING: Telling one story and without pause going into another story can imply association between the two. This can be achieved either with or without narrative bridges by grouping stories in succession.

Examples: 1. The charges against the Nixon Administration were handled this way almost on a nightly basis. The President's taxes, the break-in at Daniel Ellsberg's psychiatrist's office, Don Segretti, the Vesco case, all ran together in associated style.

2. While Phnom Penh was being surrounded and South Vietnam was falling, CBS Evening News of March 26,1975 opened with neither, but with a "group" of economic stories: the tax bill, the farm bill, and the evening stock report. This was followed by a break for a commercial as the grouping ended. It made the impression that the three stories were one story—and the most important story of the day.

Y. ACCEPTANCE OF EDITORIALS: It has become an accepted fact that network news will have an editorial. But why? Why should an editorial view be placed on a *news* program? Why is it not possible for the audience to find out the news *without* hearing an editorial?

Example: NBC and CBS incorporated their editorials within the context of the news programming, which made it most impractical for a viewer to turn the television audio down and then up again just in time to catch the next piece of news. ABC uses a better method of placing its editorials at the end of the program, much like a newspaper editorial, which can be read or simply be left unread.

Z. REPETITION: This is the simplest and oldest technique of any medium that wishes to propagandize a point of view. It was inherited from ages past and has never been used more strikingly or more effectively than it has in television newscasts. When a story appears night after night with little added to the account, or if a continuing story is repeatedly given precedence over news items that are obviously more urgent in the context of the day's events, it is a safe bet that the network is setting up its own emphasis to maintain an objective, which is usually met. The creation of the most important story today, with repetition tomorrow, can truly make it important the day after tomorrow.

Example: 1. *Our* atrocities committed in Vietnam
2. Charges against the Nixon administration
3. Bad news regarding the economy
4. Charges against the intelligence-gathering community

For years, film and video techniques were used only to enhance productions for audiences that wished to be entertained; therefore, those techniques deserved to be as guarded as a magician's hat. But those techniques were being used, and at this writing are still being used, to enhance distortion for audiences that wish to be informed. As in the days of varityped contracts, the fine print of television is more important than the bold print, but too often it passes unnoticed, just as it is intended to do.

In a country that deserves to rely upon free communications and must retain them at all costs, irresponsibility has been bred by a national free press that betrays its name and achieves distortion from the privileged sanctuary of an evening newscast. From that sanctuary, newsmen cannot be called to account. They cannot be made to reveal their source, though that source may be inflicting damage upon the innocent. They do not have to face a press conference, for they are the press. They are not subject to investigative reporting, for they are the reporters.

Walter Cronkite ends the CBS Evening News with the phrase, "And that's the way it is." After the techniques of the trade have been used, some probably believe "that's the way it is." Only sometimes. More often, it is the way the network has made the day's events appear. Too often, that's the way it isn't.

6

The Nation
Is Fitted
for Bifocals

There were two great periods of boredom between the reelection of President Nixon and the fall of South Vietnam, and newscasters went through those periods with a kind of withdrawal usually associated with those undergoing treatment for narcotics addiction.

The first period was the three months from mid-January 1973 through mid-April 1973 between the return of our men who were prisoners of war and the time when charges against the administration started to take effect. The second period was the six months from mid-September 1974 through mid-March 1975 between the pardon of President Nixon and the time when Cambodia and South Vietnam started falling apart.

The second period is reserved for a later chapter, but the first period is worth examining now since it took a leading role in the ultimate resignation of the President:

The networks couldn't have started out an evening newscast by reporting that there were no American casualties in Vietnam just like the previous week and the week before that and the week before that. They had no more staged propaganda films from North Vietnam with American prisoners of war telling the President to stop bombing. There weren't any known prisoners. There wasn't any bombing. They couldn't show demonstrations against the war because there weren't any demonstrators and we weren't in a war. No American cities burning. No campus riots. No draft. No recession.

If it hadn't been for the Sioux Indians at Wounded Knee, there wouldn't have been anything, so the networks played it for all it was worth, and it wasn't worth much. After that evaporated, all that was left were pictures of women boycotting meat, which was less interesting than the Sioux. The networks were in trouble. What could you do with a story that revealed that the U.S. Census Bureau had just found out they had forgotten to count 5,300,000 Americans? And what could you do with a Presidential veto of the Rural Water and Sewers Bill?

Boredom turns a man to sex, a woman to shopping, and it drives newscasters berserk.

And so President Nixon had brought about an intolerable situation that no conscientious newscaster could permit to continue unchallenged. Without conscience, President Nixon had created a Boredom Crisis within the United States.

There were some options open to the newscasters at the time:

They could have reported the continual violation of the Paris Accords by the North Vietnamese and the implications that could arise from their unchecked aggression. Rejected.

They could have reported the build-up of arms being supplied to the North Vietnamese by Moscow and Peking. Rejected.

They could have reported the decline in American balance of power vis-á-vis the Soviet Union. Rejected.

They could have pursued the Watergate bugging. Accepted.

And so Americans were given a point of focus.

The perception of the world's priorities was given to over 50 million Americans by the decision of those who managed CBS, NBC, and ABC.

The only way Americans would have known that the networks were setting their own priorities was if other national media had been giving different priorities than had been set by the networks.

Fortunately for the networks and unfortunately for the American audience, the other chief sources of national news communications made similar decisions of story rejection and acceptance, since there was no philosophic or political competition from those organizations. *Time* magazine, *Newsweek* magazine, *The New York Times* and *The Washington Post* followed the same stories as the networks. *Time* and *Newsweek* are distributed nationally, and though *The New York Times* and *The Washington Post* appear to be local, they have a national reach. *The New York Times Service* and the services of *The Washington Post-Los Angeles Times* have a combined subscriber list servicing some 750 local newspapers throughout the country. What often appears to be a local newspaper's independent story is no more than a reprint from one of those services. In addition, Washington correspondents the world over start their day by reading *The New York Times* and *The Washington Post,* and their stories are often generated by that reading.

All of these giant news organizations operate geographically and philosophically from the New York–Washington media cabal. It is true that the networks and national publications appear to run stories from "everywhere," but what is viewed, heard, and read is most often the *New York–Washington perception* of stories from everywhere.

It isn't the schoolbook controversy in Kanawha County of West Virginia that reaches the national audience—it is the New York–Washington perception of the schoolbook controversy. The who, what, where, when, why, and how is viewed through the prism of what is right and what is wrong, as focused by the New York–Washington ophthalmologists of communication.

Time magazine of July 8, 1974 argued against the claim of a consistent liberal bias in the New York–Washington coalition and stated that, "during much of the Vietnam war, there were significant editorial differences [among the three networks, *Time, Newsweek, The New York Times* and *The Washington Post*]. In 1972 the *Times* supported George McGovern, while *Time, Inc.* endorsed Nixon—[some endoresement!] Among *Times* columnists last year [in 1973], Tom Wicker and Anthony Lewis were more critical of Spiro Agnew than their colleague James Reston was. [Is the *degree* of criticism a reasonable claim to balance?] Further, the liberals—however that term is defined—hardly have a news monopoly, even in New York and Washington. *U.S. News and World Report* generally takes a conservative line [never within the context of the news, but only on its back page/s editorial], and *The Washington Star-News* is to the *Post's* right." [Again, a "degree" balance, and who *wouldn't* be to the *Post's* right?]

As President Harry S. Truman was nearing the end of his second term he wrote to a friend, "I really look with commiseration over the great body of my fellow citizens who, reading newspapers, live and die in the belief that they have known something of what has been passing in the world in their time."

Arthur Schlesinger, Jr. of the Kennedy administration remarked about press reports: "Their relationship to reality is often less than the shadows in Plato's cave."

Dean Rusk, Secretary of State for the Kennedy and Johnson administrations said, "Let's get rid of this genial myth of the fourth estate . . .

You [American Society of Newspaper Editors] speak to the American people, not for them . . . That this should be so would seem to be elementary, because the American people have nothing to say about who are to be publishers and editors and reporters and columnists. We cannot admit in our constitutional system room for something called a 'fourth estate', which has no democratic base."

Jack Anderson is fond of quoting Thomas Jefferson making his pre-Presidential statement: "If I had to choose between a government without newspapers and newspapers without a government, I would pick the latter." Anderson never quotes Thomas Jefferson making his post-Presidential statement: "Nothing can now be believed which is seen in a newspaper." (Frankly, I don't particularly like governments or newspapers, but if I had to have one, I would want to have both.)

By this time, everyone is familiar with *The Washington Post* through its revelations regarding the Nixon administration. "But," some would say, "that isn't the New York–Washington cabal bias—it's the truth." Much of it was; much of it was not. Many innocent people were packed together to have their lives ruined by biased reporting.

The combination of selective truth and non-truth was not enough, however, to successfully create a climate of national opinion that would cry for the administration's explusion. There was necessity to inject bias into smaller surrounding stories that collectively would achieve the desired climate in an instinctive alliance with the electronic medium.

It is not important to go through the daily repertoire of printed bias, but it is important to review the ways in which an attempt to delude the public was made and the manner in which the national press complemented the television networks in permeating the nation with diverse showers designed to gather into a single storm.

REPORTAGE: In early 1973, *The New York Times* editorially appraised the Nixon administration as "a reversion to the do-nothing Federal Government and every man-for-himself ideology of the Hoover era . . . solace to those who want to forget about the miseries of the poor, on welfare, out of work, or in dead-ends jobs." The *Times* further stated: "Nixon has repeated the dominant theme of his inaugural address, his budget, and his economic report: Social programs must now be cut back."

Objectivity: President Nixon had just requested a raise in the budget for social programs from $109 billion to $122 billion, the highest in American history.

REPORTAGE: On July 29, 1973 The *Washington Post* reprinted the first page of the President's Daily News Summary for July 13. The President's News Summary was prepared each day for President Nixon by members of the White House Staff. Alongside the reprint in the *The Washington Post* was printed the front pages of *The Washington Post* and *The New York Times* for the same date. The impression was left with the reader that the President's Daily News Summary contained only scant information about the charges against him and equally scant information about other important news stories, in contrast to the coverage given to them in *The Washington Post* and *The New York Times.*

Objectivity: The *Washington Post* failed to inform its readers that the reproduced front page of the President's Daily News Summary was merely *an index capsulization* of the stories he would find printed inside the news summary.

REPORTAGE: *The New York Times Book of the Watergate Hearings* was a day-to-day edited transcript of those hearings from the first witness forward, ending with the day of the testimony of Howard Hunt.

Objectivity: The following day Pat Buchanan testified, whom even critics of the President recognized as the witness who seriously embarrassed the President's opposition on the committee and staff, replete with documented examples of Democratic Party "dirty tricks." Pat Buchanan's testimony was not included in *The New York Times Book.*

REPORTAGE: *Time* magazine (January 2, 1974) ran a group of pictures under the heading "The White House Watergate Men", though some in the photographic gallery had not been charged by anyone with a connection to Watergate and *none* had been tried.

Objectivity: Just pages after that story, *Time* printed a photograph of a woman from a militant organization caught holding a gun in her hand. The caption ran: "Chesimard Allegedly Robbing Bank in 1971." The word "allegedly" was correct, but no such courtesy of the word was extended to those in the administration. (*Time* repeated the photographic gallery technique under the caption, "The Other Nixon Watergate Men" in its March 11, 1974 issue, again including pictures of people not charged with a connection to Watergate and none of whom had been tried.)

REPORTAGE: *Newsweek* magazine reported that John Dean would reveal to the Senate Select Committee that White House officials had planned to assassinate the President of Panama, but that the assassination plan had been dropped at the last minute. *Newsweek* not only published this report, but sent an advance press release to thousands of newspapers throughout the country.

Objectivity: The report was false and not retracted when *Newsweek* learned it was untrue.

REPORTAGE: The *Newsweek* cover of July 22, 1974 featured a bold head: "The Evidence," followed by type that embraced the cover: "I want you all to stonewall it, let them plead the Fifth Amendment, cover-up or anything else. . . " Behind the transcript was a picture of President Nixon.

Objectivity: *Newsweek*'s cover did not include the rest of the transcript, which ended, ". . . On the other hand, I would prefer that you do it the other way." (When Congressman Sandman of New Jersey referred to this out-of-context cover in his defense of the President at the impeachment inquiry, *Newsweek* failed to report his statement.)

REPORTAGE: There was extensive coverage of an out-of-context report from the House Judiciary Committee regarding a Dictabelt memorandum President Nixon used as an aide-memoire of March 21, 1974. The President started it by saying, "As far as the day was concerned it was relatively uneventful except for the talk with Dean." The out-of-context report was made without the "except for the talk with Dean" portion of the President's sentence. Most media corrected this error when they realized the House Judiciary Committee leak was out of context.

Objectivity: Although *Newsweek* magazine ran the entire transcript elsewhere, its lead article read: "An 'Uneventful' Day." "Buried elsewhere in the bulky appendices was an aide-memoire Mr. Nixon dictated the night of the 21st, remarking that it had been a mostly 'uneventful' day, rambling over Dean's disclosures and the danger that Hunt might 'blow'—and neglecting to mention the supposed investigation he later claimed to have set in motion that very afternoon . . ." Not a mention of *"except for the talk with Dean."* With these key words again omitted, the

76

impression was given that the President did not consider Dean's revelations important.

REPORTAGE: On July 26, 1974 a non-editorial page of *The Washington Post* ran an eight-column headline: "Nixon Support in Committee Appears to be Wilting." On the same page there was one other eight-column headline over another story regarding the impeachment inquiry: "Judiciary Committee Members Splendidly Rising to History."

Objectivity: Both headlines stated editorial opinions rather than news. Taken together, each one gave greater effect to the other.

REPORTAGE: *Newsweek* magazine initiated the weekly "My Turn" column to give an opportunity to those not connected with the publication to give their own views. During the first year of the existence of "My Turn", 26 columns related to the Nixon administration in a pro-or-con style.

Objectivity: Of those 26 columns, 6 supported the administration, while 20 were opposed.

REPORTAGE: The Mitchell-Stans-Vesco case was mammoth news in early 1974, with the trial concerning an alleged obstruction of justice regarding a campaign contribution from Robert Vesco allegedly in return for the Securities and Exchange Commission dropping a case against him. When the prosecution had the SEC Chairman, Mr. William Casey, on the stand, he testified that John Mitchell had never asked him to drop the case, nor had he ever talked to him about it. It developed that it was John Dean who had talked to Casey. All of this was reported as the trial commenced.

Objectivity: On Page 27 of *The New York Times* in the 38th paragraph of the story it was reported, "Mr. Dean, like every Government witness, was asked if Mr. Mitchell tried to get him to 'fix' the Vesco case, and like all the others he replied 'no'."
Absolutely crucial news for the defense. Page 27. Thirty-eighth paragraph of the story.

REPORTAGE: Victor Lasky was given critical prominence during the hearings for Nelson Rockefeller's nomination for Vice-President. A controversy developed regarding the book Victor Lasky had written on Arthur Goldberg, subsidized by Rockefeller relatives and friends. *Time* magazine wrote: "It was written by political hatchet man Victor Lasky, who had previously collected together every anti-Kennedy rumor he could find in his 1963 book, *JFK: The Man and The Myth.*"

Objectivity: What *Time* neglected to remind its readers of was that *JFK: The Man and The Myth* was a national best-seller from September through November, 1963, and that the day following President Kennedy's assassination Victor Lasky requested his publisher to take all the copies of his book off the shelves of outlets in respect to the late President.

A real hatchet man.

It might also have been in the interest of objectivity to have reminded the 1974 readers and viewers of the Rockefeller hearings that Fred Cook's 1964 book on Senator Goldwater was subsidized by the Democratic National Committee.

REPORTAGE: *Newsweek* reported mass executions taking place under the post-Allende government of Chile. One of the allegations was that the Santiago morgue had processed 2,796 bodies during the two weeks after the overthrow of Allende.

Objectivity: The figure of 2,796 bodies was the number processed by the Santiago morgue in the first nine months of the year rather than the two weeks following Allende's overthrow. The figure was comparable to that of cities of similar size. The report went uncorrected.

REPORTAGE: *The New York Times* early in 1973 headlined a story regarding U.S. Ambassador to South Vietnam Graham Martin: "An Ambassador's Advice: Forget About Honesty". *The Washington Post* reported the story as well, both newspapers quoting a cable from Ambassador Martin to the State Department in which he said, " . . . It would be the height of folly to permit [Senator Edward M.] Kennedy, whose staff will spearhead this effort [to reduce Vietnam aid] the tactical advantage of honest and detailed answers to questions raised in his [Senator Kennedy's] letter." Months later, *Newsweek* reprinted the cable in the same manner.

Objectivity: The cable went on to read: "While, as an individual senator he has the right to raise them, they are not questions which either fall within the purview of his subcommittee or which should be answered to him as an individual senator so close before the full administration position is presented to the Foreign Affairs and the Foreign Relations Committees." None of the publications listed above quoted this continuation of the cable or subsequent portions that recommended that Senator Kennedy be informed of his (Ambassador Martin's) thinking and that Senator Kennedy's inquiries would be covered fully by executive testimony before the Senate and House committees under whose purview the subject was assigned.

REPORTAGE: *Time* magazine of May 20, 1974 reported that "Leslie Dutton, a Nixon loyalist from Santa Monica (Cal.) who only two weeks ago was posing with Nixon in the Oval Office after giving him a petition of support from 10,000 admirers, confessed (sic): 'We've got to start thinking about the welfare of the party, and where this leaves the President I just don't know.' " After reading the report, Mrs. Dutton wrote *Time:*

Dear Sir:
I very strongly object to your story in the May 20, 1974, issue of *Time* magazine where your reporter in Los Angeles, Mr. Leo Janos, quoted me as he described it 'confessing.' The remarks printed in *Time* magazine were totally inaccurate and misrepresentative of what I actually said. The entire statement attributed to me was incorrect and it gave the direct impression that I no longer supported the President, which is the worst and most despicable type of reporting and does not best serve the image of the journalistic profession.
I stand very much behind President Nixon and the Presidency. I am busy working for the Republican Party here in California and I am, as well as all others, concerned about the treatment of the case now before the Judiciary Committee.
In all fairness to the 1700 supporters whom I represented during the presentation of our 40-foot scroll to the President I demand that you set the record straight.

Very truly yours,
Mrs. Leslie Dutton

Objectivity: Unfortunately, *Time* did not print Mrs. Dutton's letter.

There was much the national media chose not to print, show, or tell (some of which is mentioned in the following chapter). Perhaps the media were too concerned with what they considered to be more important stories that took priority in the editing process. Consider, at the time of the impeachment advocacy, the importance of *The Washington Post* article headlined:

PRESIDENT EXCEEDS GAS LIMIT

President Nixon and his entourage have used at least 170 gallons of gasoline for pleasure driving during the President's 18-day stay in Southern California.

A compilation based on the President's announced travel and on a conservative estimate of his drive on unannounced trips with C. G. (Bebe) Rebozo shows that Mr. Nixon himself has driven about 500 miles in his late-model Lincoln limousine. According to figures of the Environmental Protection Agency, Lincoln limousines get 7.9 miles to the gallon.

This would mean that the presidential car has consumed 62 gallons in his drives around Southern California.

Mr. Nixon has been accompanied on all of his drives by Secret Service agents in a late-model station wagon, which also gets about eight miles to the gallon. At least three other presidential cars made the 125-mile trip from the President's oceanside San Clemente estate to Palm Desert, where Mr. Nixon has been the guest since Wednesday of publishing magnate Walter Annenberg, the U.S. ambassador to Great Britain.

The fuel-use estimate is based upon eight miles a gallon for the 500 miles driven both by the President and the Secret Service station wagon and 11 miles to the gallon for the three other cars that also accompanied Mr. Nixon from the airport to San Clemente.

Mr. Nixon's announced drives, in addition to the Palm Desert trip, have included a 106-mile round trip to La Jolla to attend the wedding of his physician, Dr. Walter Tkach, and shorter drives last Sunday to the San Clemente Presbyterian Church and to a Mexican restaurant for dinner.

However, White House officials confirmed privately that Mr. Nixon had taken six unannounced drives with Rebozo. One was a very short drive and the others were drives of two to three hours apiece.

According to one White House official, one of the unannounced drives proceeded from the presidential compound to the White House press message center 13 miles away in Laguna Beach without being noticed by any reporters.

On these private drives Rebozo usually takes the wheel with the President alongside in the front seat . . . .

Wow!

When there was no charge available to level against President Nixon, masters of trivia invented one with the implication that everything President Nixon did was somehow wrong.

80

President Nixon had made known that he was planning the California trip cited by *The Washington Post,* and he was soundly criticized at the time because, many reported, he would waste a precious amount of fuel if he used Air Force One for the journey. When he traveled to California by a commercial jet, he was then criticized for not giving the press the consideration of traveling with him aboard the plane and for his neglect of security hazards.

With such biased communications, no one in the national audience could retain 20-20 vision. The bifocals made to watch television and also allow reading of the national press were ground from the same East Coast prescription. It just goes to prove that this nation needed a damned good ophthalmologist. Maybe someone in Des Moines.

7

The Un-News

In the Soviet Union, if they don't like something, they simply act as though it had never happened.

In the early 1960s they decided Stalin had never happened. They took his body out of its Red Square tomb, buried it on the other side of the Kremlin wall, tore down every statue of his likeness, and eliminated his name in quickly reprinted history books. In no time at all, Stalin was a non-person. In the mid-1960s the Soviet Union ignored the space accomplishments of the United States and, by ignoring them, turned them into non-events. In the early 1970's Solzhenitsyn's *Gulag Archipelago* was a non-book. Within their system, non-persons, non-events, and non-books run invisibly rampant.

It can't happen here, we all thought. But it did. Like Stalin, space capsules, and Solzhenitsyn, some American persons, events, and books became non-persons, non-events, and non-books.

Although every facet of Gerald Ford's and Nelson Rockefeller's lives was probed and investigated after their nominations to become one heartbeat away from the Presidency, Carl Albert, who *was* one heartbeat away from the Presidency during those two lengthy periods, was ignored by the national media. No investigative reporting. No television documentaries. No probing major newspaper profiles. A non-person.

Although Peter Rodino, Chairman of the House Committee on the

Judiciary, probed every facet of President Nixon's finances, Rodino refused to disclose his own net worth. While he received $14,000 in interest in 1972 (at 6% this would be interest on nearly a quarter of a million dollars), no one cared enough to investigate what funds created that interest. A non-event.

The Institute for American Strategy held a press conference in late October 1974 to announce publication of its $300,000 study by 18 scholars headed by Dr. Ernest W. Lefever, Senior Fellow in Foreign Policy Studies at the Brookings Institution. The study (referred to in Chapter Three) was titled "TV and National Defense: An Analysis of CBS News, 1972-1973". The study came to the conclusion that CBS was an active advocate of a position that implied or called for a lesser commitment to American allies and to lower defense expenditures. None of the three networks mentioned the press conference or reported its findings or the fact that the study had taken place or that the book was published. A non-book.

It is regrettable that during those years some entrepreneur didn't initiate the U.S. Evening Un-News, in which the program could have informed the nation of those stories of interest that most other national news sources thought unworthy of bringing to national attention.

Beyond the ignored and obvious stories of North Vietnam's steady build-up with weapons supplied by Moscow and Peking, there were ignored and obvious stories that would have put events into their authentic domestic political context. Had those stories been given their justified prominence, the climate of those years surely would have changed. Had the techniques utilized by the nation's prime communicators also been employed to enhance the domestic political Un-News, American political history would today be radically different.

It is doubtful that most Americans will recall the following stories. Since they were detrimental to the communicators' prime cause, they were left to die as soon as they were born. Some were killed. They all ended up in the wastebasket of Un-News.

UN-NEWS: The Associated Press Wire Service of April 18, 1974, at the time President Nixon was directed to pay back taxes on "airplane tickets" for members of his family when they had flown with him on the Presidential aircraft, "The Spirit of '76," (Air Force One):

> While Congress is in recess, nearly four dozen senators and representatives are traveling overseas at taxpayer expense—"feeding at the trough" as one State Department official put it. Many are accompanied by their wives.

The legislators are members of delegations to international conferences in Romania, Malaysia, Korea and Taiwan.

Their itineraries also include stops in Paris, Athens, Istanbul, Singapore and Hong Kong. They travel in Air Force planes, and at each stop are eligible for $75 a day spending money.

On two of the trips, the congressional delegations will meet with legislators from other countries to "talk and pass resolutions on international topics of the day," said the State Department official who asked not to be named. A third group will look on as observers while outgoing Treasury Secretary George P. Shultz participates in the annual meeting of the Asian Development Bank in Kuala Lumpur, Malaysia.

On all three trips, some wives are going along "for protocol reasons," said an aide to Rep. Melvin Price, D-Ill. Price and his wife are part of a 50-person delegation headed by House Majority Leader Thomas P. "Tip" O'Neill, D-Mass., attending interparliamentary conferences in South Korea and Taiwan.

O'Neill is traveling with both his wife and daughter. His daughter, Rosemary, works for the State Department and serves as an escort for the traveling congressmen, a department official said.

The State Department handles arrangements for most overseas trips but refers all queries concerning itineraries to Capitol Hill. "I've been instructed not to discuss congressional travel," said Elizabeth Burke, head of the Department's congressional travel section.

Asked why the State Department would not release unclassified information relating to travel at public expense, another department official explained that "their first allegiance is to the congressmen, and you don't want to be running around advertising that your principals are feeding at the trough."

Members of the O'Neill delegation are stopping off for two days in Hong Kong, with the option of a side trip to Saigon, on the way to South Korea and Taiwan. Rep. Morris K. Udall, D-Ariz., and his wife went along because "Mo thought it'd be a fun trip," an aide said.

UN-NEWS: A UPI dispatch of June 25, 1974:

In a 21-17 party line vote, the House Judiciary Committee today killed a motion to subpoena House records on campaign contributions given members of congress by milk producers in 1970-71 . . . All 21 Democrats opposed the motion of Rep. Wiley Mayne, R-Iowa, and all 17 Republicans supported it. One of the allegations against Nixon in the impeachment inquiry is that he was influenced in raising dairy price supports by a $2 million campaign pledge from milk producers. Nixon argued he was under congressional pressure to meet dairymen's demands. Mayne said 154 members of congress co-sponsored legislation to force higher price supports, but committee chairman Peter W. Rodino Jr., D-N.J., said the committee has no authority to investigate what motivates congressmen to back legislation.

Congressman Mayne argued that it would be "unfair for men to sit in judgment of President Nixon after having done substantially the same thing." He said that President Nixon might have vetoed such a bill if Congressmen Mills and Albert hadn't led such an effective lobbying effort and that it would be a "double standard" for Congress to condemn the President for what Congress had demanded.

UN-NEWS: The Tower Amendment of early April 1974 was defeated. Senator Tower suggested that every member of Congress send a copy of his federal income tax return to the Joint Committee on Internal Revenue and Taxation for audit and, if discrepancies were found, the member of Congress and the IRS would be simultaneously notified. Senator Tower's reasoning was that if President Nixon was subjected to this kind of scrutiny, Congress should meet the same criterion. Senator Kennedy was opposed to this. So was Tip O'Neill. So was Bella Abzug. So was Elizabeth Holtzman. (Other than in a column by Nick Thimmesch, the easily defeated Tower Amendment was hardly made public.)

UN-NEWS: There was a great deal of television coverage given to the controversy as to whether the Mid-East alert of October 1973 was justified or was contrived to divert the nation's interest from the charges against President Nixon. However, on April 9, 1974 the House of Representatives voted to end all further inquiry into the matter since Congressman Thomas Morgan, Chairman of the Foreign Affairs Committee, and Congressman John Buchanan had examined the text of Chairman Brezhnev's message to President Nixon during that crisis period. "I'm satisfied that the alert was justified," Congressman Morgan said with Congressman Buchanan's agreement. They filed a report with the Foreign Affairs Committee and the committee voted 26 to 2 to recommend that the House not adopt a formal resolution of inquiry, which had been previously recommended. The House of Representatives agreed with their assessment.

UN-NEWS: When President Nixon was being blamed for the energy crisis of 1974, no network analyst reminded his audience that President Nixon had advocated energy legislation on June 4, 1971 when energy was not a national issue. He submitted a 12-page message to Congress that was ignored.

A United Press International dispatch of June 28, 1974:

Sen. Hubert H. Humphrey, D-Minn., says if any corporations contributed illegally to his 1972 presidential bid he "was unaware of it."

The former Vice President and 1968 Democratic presidential nominee was accused along with Rep. Wilbur D. Mills, D-Ark., of accepting illegal corporate gifts in a draft report prepared for the Senate Watergate Committee. The report also said both their campaign managers invoked the 5th Amendment to avoid testifying.

"I have not seen this draft report, but according to information made public by the press it is filled with innuendoes and inaccuracies," Humphrey said in a two-page statement Thursday.

Humphrey said he had not cooperated with the Watergate Committee's investigation of an alleged $25,000 donation from the Associated Milk Producers, Inc. (AMPI) because he did not know about the gift.

He said his personal expenditures during his try for the 1972 nomination came from a trust fund he established in 1965.

The report charged that Jack Chestnut, Humphrey's former campaign manager, destroyed the campaign's financial records for the period before April 7, 1972, when a new full disclosure law went into effect.

[Jack Chestnut was convicted in New York on May 8, 1975 for illegal acceptance of campaign funds, according to a two-sentence item on CBS Evening News, 24 minutes into the broadcast. He was sentenced on June 26, 1975; a one sentence item on the CBS Evening News, seventeen minutes into the broadcast. Although the case was comparable to the Mitchell-Stans-Vesco case, and Humphrey was called as a witness, it was unimportant because it was *not made* important by the news communicators.]

The report charged that Minnesota Mining and Manufacturing, Inc. (3M) illegally contributed $1,000 to Humphrey in corporate funds channeled through a consultant in Europe.

Humphrey said he received 10 checks of $100 each from individuals, and "If these individuals were reimbursed with corporate funds, I was not aware of it."

Humphrey also said his office had provided more than 200 documents requested by the Committee.

Un-News: Associated Press, June 28, 1974:

. . . the [Senate Select] Committee staff on Thursday circulated a new report dealing with presidential campaign finances of Democrats George McGovern and John V. Lindsay.

It said that McGovern is campaigning for re-election to the Senate this year with the aid of $340,417 in left-over 1972 presidential funds. It said he shifted these funds out of presidential campaign committees while these committees were forcing creditors to write off $35,322 as bad debts. The transfer of funds from one campaign to another has been used in the past by other candidates and the report did not challenge its legality.

But it said the maneuver raises a question of whether McGovern violated at least the spirit of the federal law banning corporate gifts to federal candidates.

A McGovern spokesman, John Holum, said the left-over presidential money was shifted to the Senate race on the orders of several state and local presidential finance chairmen who controlled the money. Holum said McGovern would try to keep the senators on the Watergate Committee from adopting the staff's findings.

The report said $10,000 in cash was raised for former New York Mayor Lindsay's presidential campaign by a city Highway Department official who solicited the money from two contractors who later got a $1.7 million job to supply the city with asphalt.

It said the money, in $20 bills stuffed into an envelope, passed through the hands of Lindsay's top campaign aide, Richard Aurelio, and cannot be accounted for.

Aurelio responded by calling the report an example of "sloppy reporting by the committee staff" and said all the cash had been properly recorded and reported publicly. This directly contradicted the committee staff's findings, which said a review of Lindsay finance records "fails to reveal any recording of the cash contributions."

UN-NEWS: After Vice President Agnew's resignation, Senator Barry Goldwater was interviewed on NBC's "Meet the Press". His candid statement regarding the Senate put events into perspective for the Sunday viewer, but it was not given any major attention by the media. It died, and there was no follow-up investigative reporting:

MR. SPIVAK: Now, while we are on that, I would like to quote something else you said and that is that there is not a man in the Senate who couldn't be gotten on charges similar to those leveled against former Vice President Agnew if somebody wanted to make out a case about their campaign donations.

Now, did you say that?

SENATOR GOLDWATER: Yes, I said that and I mean it.

MR. SPIVAK: Would you tell us what you meant by that?

SENATOR GOLDWATER: There is not a one of us who has run for office who hasn't been given money. We have to have money to run.

Now, usually this money is gathered by a committee headed by a friend who is chairman, but inevitably there comes that time or times when a man will say, "Well, if I am going to give him money, I want to hand it over myself."

So let's say some friend, or supposed friend, or man I don't even know, comes in my office and hands me a check or hands me some money. And then later on, in an effort to get me someone who knew that that man was in my office and gave that money, to get that man—say the Internal Revenue got something on him—not bad, but enough so that it could worry the man, and he was told, "Look, if you will do this, we will do that." So he is willing to make a statement that "Yes, I gave Goldwater a thousand dollars and I got a favor out of him."

This is what I was referring to and every one of us in public life, or every one that I know, has had experiences that could be turned in, not necessarily to the resulting Agnew experience, but to the experience that he was going through at that particular time.

UN-NEWS: A week after President Nixon's pardon, the Republican National Committee passed a resolution commending President Nixon for his achievements. It declared that he had "accomplished much during his Presidency, particularly in the field of foreign affairs, as he strived to assure a generation of peace" and that "these remarkable accomplishments will be treated kindly by history."

UN-NEWS: Investigative reporting was nonexistent when it came to the partisanship of Archibald Cox or the operating procedures of Judge Sirica. One would think non-partisanship would be vital for the position of the Special Prosecutor. Ethical operating procedures, one would believe, would be vital for a judge.

Two weeks prior to Archibald Cox's appointment as Special Prosecutor he was reported in an interview as follows: ". . . Cox said he had such sharp 'philosophical and ideological' differences with the administration's Justice Department operation that he could not consider taking a job with the department. . . . He made caustic criticisms of former Attorney General Mitchell whom he had described earlier as 'insensitive to the importance of [civil] liberties.' He then went on to criticize President Nixon, Kleindienst, and policies of the Justice Department in general. Citing his administration criticisms, Cox emphatically rejected any notion of taking a Justice Department job. . . ."

Archibald Cox had been John Kennedy's task force director for position papers in the 1960 campaign, served as the Solicitor General in Robert Kennedy's Justice Department, and retained that position in the Johnson administration. In 1972 he was an alternate delegate to the Massachusetts State Democratic Convention, pledged to Senator Edmund Muskie.

His appointees included Henry Ruth, who was to become the Special Prosecutor after Leon Jaworski's resignation. Ruth had served under

Robert Kennedy within the Justice Department and left John Lindsay's cabinet to join Cox. James Vorenberg, another top Cox appointee, served as Special Assistant to Attorney General Ramsey Clark and served as the head of a campaign task force on crime for candidate George McGovern. Another Cox appointee, William Merrill, had run as a Democratic candidate for Congress. Of the 11 senior staff members of the Special Prosecution Force, seven had been appointees of Robert Kennedy. Only one was a Republican. Most retained their positions on the Special Prosecution Force after Cox's departure.

Although Judge Sirica was honored as *Time* magazine's Man of the Year, and was acclaimed by the national media, his rate of reversal in the Court of Appeals was among the highest of the District Court judges. Joseph L. Rauh, Jr. of the American Civil Liberties Union said, "It seems ironic that those most opposed to Mr. Nixon's lifetime espousal of ends justifying means should now make a hero of a judge who practiced this formula to the detriment of a fair trial for the Watergate Seven." *The Washingtonion Magazine,* which was opposed to President Nixon during the "Watergate" crisis and was generally favorably disposed to liberal thought, included Judge Sirica on its list of judges who should be removed from the bench, basing judgment on "Sirica's careless legal errors, his short temper, his inattentiveness to court proceedings, his misguided view of the purpose of judicial power, his lack of compassion for his fellow human beings, and, strange as it now seems, his lack of interest in the truth." In the "Watergate" case, Sirica "badgered, accused, and castigated witnesses, prosecutors, and defense lawyers. He read transcripts of confidential bench conferences to the jury. He used the threat of lengthy sentences to force defendants into abandoning their constitutional rights. He turned the trial into an inquisition, and justice into a charade."

Louis Nizer, the distinguished attorney and author, stated:

> . . . by what means did Judge Sirica achieve the unraveling for which he deserves great credit? The objective was magnificent—the exposure of the Watergate scandal. But how? Five defendants pleaded guilty to burglary. Two others stood trial and were convicted. He told them that they knew more than they had told and he was sentencing them provisionally to 35–40 years. If they cooperated and confessed all, he would reconsider the punishment. After four weeks of reflecting on the difference between almost a life sentence of 35 years and maybe a year or two sentence, which they ultimately received, one of the defendants cracked, and wrote a letter to him saying he was ready to talk. Thus, the great objective was achieved.
>
> Now do we want judges, despite the wonderful result in this case to use

penalties to force people to surrender their right under the Fifth Amendment not to talk? Is this not a form of judicial duress? Is it very different, except in degree and kind, from other forms of duress to obtain confessions, which our Supreme Court has repeatedly condemned? In one case in which a murderer was forced to confess, giving objective evidence which left no doubt of his guilt, the Supreme Court set aside the conviction and freed him. Justice Douglas wrote the following sentence, which I have always admired for its forthrightness. He said that it was true that some murderers who now go free would be caught if third degree methods were used to wring confessions from them. But "this is the price we pay for a civilized society." For if we resort to duress, then sooner or later innocent men are going to be pounded and beaten. There are many forms of duress. Some are subtle, not merely the rubber pipe applied below the face to leave no marks, but endless questioning which deprives the victim of sleep, and other psychological devices. If once we break down the constitutional guarantees, we set an evil precedent. The good result obtained by Judge Sirica is not enough. If we want to keep our political life purified, we must look at the means by which Judge Sirica's triumph was achieved . . .

Although Nizer's statements were included in a major address to the New York University Law School, not a word was repeated in a national newscast.

UN-NEWS: After the discharge of Archibald Cox, the networks did not reveal where the "spontaneous outpouring" of anti-Nixon telegrams was coming from. The staff of Senator William Scott of Virginia took a tally and discovered that 77% of the impeachment telegrams coming to his office were sent by people who had supported George McGovern in 1972. Thus, the networks ignored what could have been a major story: that the calls for impeachment at the time might not at all have been representative, but could have largely reflected the partisanship of those who had supported the defeated candidate of 1972.

UN-NEWS: None of the three networks reported *Common Cause's* organizational efforts in phoning throughout the country urging that telegrams and letters be sent to the Congress against the President and supporting legislation for an independent prosecutor No national news organization investigated to find out why Archibald Cox held a meeting with John Gardner, the Director of *Common Cause,* shortly after Cox's dismissal.

UN-NEWS: When President Nixon first agreed to turn over the tapes of Presidential conversations, one was played at a Georgetown cocktail party. This was reported by national news organizations, but there were no national follow-up stories on the man, William Dobrovir, an employee of Ralph Nader, who illegally played that Presidential tape at the party.

He went on to lobby among the members of Congress for the impeachment of President Nixon for high crimes and misdemeanors.

Although many in the national media considered President Nixon responsible for the actions of his subordinates, none held Ralph Nader responsible for the actions of his staff member.

UN-NEWS: Major news organizations did not check into who was financing the advertising campaign by the American Civil Liberties Union calling for President Nixon's impeachment. Similarly, no major news organization reported that, when persons phoned the Democratic National Committee to inquire about impeachment, the DNC urged them to contact the American Civil Liberties Union and to assist the ACLU in its efforts.

UN-NEWS: Though relatively unknown congressmen were given national attention on the networks when they advocated the impeachment of President Nixon, none of the three networks reported, during the height of the impeachment controversy, the words of the former Speaker of the House, Democrat John McCormack:

> Impeachment of the President would have a serious blow upon the national interests of the United States and that's my country—our country . . . We're not Democrats or Republicans when we consider the national interests of our country. The national interest is paramount. These are my views as an American. I see no evidence justifying impeachment yet. And if I was Speaker, even if I felt there was, I'd have to pass upon the additional question: Do I think impeachment would help or hurt my country? I'd have that additional question to pass upon. So far as the President resigning is concerned, all I can say is that I hope he will not.

UN-NEWS: In 1974 it was revealed that Bill Moyers, the former Press Secretary to President Johnson who exhibited continual public horror at the so-called dirty tricks of the Nixon administration, had requested the FBI to collect derogatory data about aides to Senator Goldwater at the time of the 1964 Presidential campaign between Johnson and Goldwater. Two weeks prior to the election, while he was Special Assistant to President Johnson, Moyers asked the FBI to run a check on 15 members of the Goldwater staff.

UN-NEWS: The House of Representatives increased their expense allowances by $9280 per member during the inflationary year of 1974. The networks didn't report it. On October 18, 1974, Robert Pear of *The Washington Star-News,* not a national publication, did:

> The House of Representatives has increased expense allowances by a total of more than $9,000 per member in the past year without formal debate, much less a vote, by the full house.
>
> Of the total, $2,250 is earmarked for the stationery allowance. But since the money can be used for any purpose a congressman desires, some members have described it as an official pay raise.
>
> The increases, ordered by the Committee on House Administration, came to light as congressmen returned home to decry inflation and campaign for re-election.
>
> The total of allowances in six different categories rose from $16,560 to $25,840, a difference of $9,280.
>
> Rep. William Dickinson of Alabama, ranking Republican on the committee, said the action of the House in 1971, giving the panel authority to set expense allowances, permitted a "rip-off." Without a requirement to bring the issue to the floor, he said yesterday, members "just laugh and chortle and pass the goodies." He said there was "no responsibility and no culpability" in the absence of roll-call votes.
>
> "I think we've gone too far with some of these allowances," Rep. Thomas S. Gettys of South Carolina said in an interview just off the floor of the House. The timing was unfortunate, he said, since federal agencies were supposed to be holding down expenses in the effort to fight inflation. . . .
>
> Gettys called for revision of the current piecemeal system of House allowances, which he described as "archaic." His frugality has brought good-natured teasing from his colleagues, who he says might give away the statue atop the Capitol without his restraint.
>
> Others who reportedly opposed some of the allowance increases were Reps. Samuel L. Devine of Ohio and John H. Ware of Pennsylvania, both Republicans.
>
> Even with the increases, Thompson said, "literally dozens of members come to me pleading they don't have enough money for stationery, phones and staff."
>
> A spokesman for D.C. Dem. Walter E. Fauntroy said the squeeze in his office was particularly tight because he had more constituents than live in any congressman's district. In addition, "the people are right here—they don't have to make a long-distance call," the spokesman said.

UN-NEWS: Although the networks seemed to report every word of Archibald Cox, they reported only those words that enhanced their own views. None of the three networks reported his comments made in Concord on February 18, 1974:

> The media certainly is turning gradually to a more active role in shaping the course of events through their news columns and commentaries as well as on their editorial pages. It isn't true of smaller papers around the country, but I think it's true of *The Washington Post, The New York Times, Newsweek,* and a number of big papers, and I rather think it seems to be true of some of the network presentations. It does seem to me that the selection of items emphasized often reflects the sort of a notion that the press is the fourth branch of government, and it should play a major role in government. I'm not so sure that I want it that way when there are only three networks—to me that's an awful lot of power to give to whomever runs the three networks.

He went on to say:

> I have no grounds to complain about the way the media has treated me. Indeed, they've treated me better than I deserved.

UN-NEWS: It was widely reported that criminal indictments resulted from illegal campaign contributions raised by the Committee for the Re-Election of the President. According to *The Washington Monthly,* while less than 2% of the money received resulted in such indictments, approximately 15% of the money received for Wilbur Mills' campaign was proven to be illegal corporate gifts. A contributing lobbyist, at the behest of Mills, intervened with the I.R.S. "to stop massive tax investigations of several big shoe companies" and, according to *The Wall Street Journal* in a story not picked up by the networks, the decision cost the public some $100 million in uncollected taxes.

UN-NEWS: None of the three networks reported the story of Frank von Riper in *The New York Daily News* of April 25, 1975 revealing that a then-new statute of limitations included in the recently signed Campaign Reform Bill would prohibit the prosecution of Democrat Congressman Wilbur Mills and Democratic National Chairman Robert Strauss for alleged fund-raising violations. Although they were under investigation, they were now "free of charges" since the statute of limitations, which was to have run for five years, had been "changed" to run for only three years.

A portion of the bill stated: "No person shall be prosecuted, tried or punished for a violation (or the fact) unless the indictment is found, or the information is instituted within three years after the date of the violation." Thus, although the indictments of Nixon administration officials had already been achieved, those Democrats who were under investigation, supposedly to "be dealt with after the 'Watergate' matter was taken care of," were safe as of January 1, 1975.

Two days prior to the law's taking effect, Ashland Oil, Inc., from which Strauss accepted a $50,000 cash contribution, pleaded guilty to five counts of making illegal cash contributions to political campaigns. The year before, Ashland Oil and its president had been fined for illegally contributing $100,000 to the 1972 Nixon campaign.

Walter Lippman once wrote: "The power to determine each day what shall seem important and shall be neglected is a power unlike any that has been exercised since the Pope lost his hold on the secular mind." That power is best reflected in the double standard of headlining stories against the media's philosophic opponents and omitting stories that could have brought a negative public response toward the media's own philosophical allies.

The country was not allowed to see the whole political story in context and perspective.

In a more personal sense, the double standard caused many good people from the Committee for the Re-Election of the President to receive wide media attention and therefore to be summoned to appear before the Special Prosecution Force to answer charges at great personal cost in reputation and finances. At the same time, more powerful national figures whose political philosophy synchronized with that of the national media reveled in their immunity, and some became national heroes. Peter Rodino, Chairman of the Committee on the Judiciary, did not have to answer for the $30,923 received from labor contributions. Wilbur Mills, in addition to irregularities regarding campaign financing, did not have to answer for labor contributions in the sum of $90,000. No one with the power to bring national attention to those facts undertook to do so.

Eric Sevareid totally ignored the fact that Wilbur Mills had spent $1700 in cash in one night at the Silver Slipper when Sevareid defended Mills in his CBS Network commentary of October 15, 1974 in the midst of Mills' campaign for reelection against the conservative Republican, Judy Petty.

THE UNINTENTIONAL UNMAKING OF THE UN-NEWS: The Mills incident, of course, was unique. It was meant to have been un-news, but ironically Larry Krebbs, a cameraman employed by a local Washington D.C. television station (WMAL) was listening to his police radio in his car and heard that an incident was occurring at the Tidal Basin. Larry Krebbs hurried over there hoping to catch the event. He did.

Larry Krebbs' report could not be ignored, although it took days for its revelation to the public. CBS finally relegated the discovery of the incident to a short segment following 17 minutes of its network news program.

When it came to Wilbur Mills, Eric Sevareid made an abrupt about-face on his feelings regarding the way public personages should handle the press:

> ... Maybe Mills just got fed up, like Wrong-Way Corrigan or that driver of the wayward bus who just headed for Florida. Someone once said people can be classified as life-enhancers or lawnmowers or well-poisoners. Mr. Mills was a lawnmower, back and forth, office to home, home to office, year after year: the job, family, duty. So maybe he looked at the morning sky one day while stuffing the old briefcase and realized the years were just about gone. The days of wine and roses that never were, never would be. If he went a bit berserk, he's got the silent sympathy of millions of others of similar age and history. But the press won't allow it. He broke their sacred category rule. There is a device for a public man to use in dealing with the press concerning his private life. He can say, and many used to, what Secretary of Defense Schlesinger said to the reporter who asked him about his religious conversion. "None of your damned business," he said.

Every one knew that Larry Krebbs, the Channel Seven cameraman, would not be awarded a Pulitzer Prize for his quick action and his unique report. But he certainly deserved something. At least, perhaps, a bottle of the Un-Cola.

8

The Day of the Tarnished Emmy

Unlike the death of a President, the flags were not lowered to half-staff, nor were bridges renamed, nor were plaques engraved, nor were chisels in sculptors' hands hurrying to make his likeness in blocks of stone.

But as in the death of a President, the Administration was over in mid-term, grieved people were crying in the East Room, and the South Lawn might as well have been Arlington Cemetery. Not a casket to go beneath ground. A helicopter to rise above ground, to scatter the grass, to move into the gray sky as viewers strained to follow what fast became no more than a dot lost behind a mass of trees. The assemblage silently walked back to their offices out of a need of destination rather than a sense of reason. On their desks were piles of work they had planned to accomplish tomorrow, but instead those piles were to be packed in boxes to become another part of yesterday. While the co-workers sat stunned in their offices, an unknown "they" removed his portraits from the corridor walls.

The climate was complete and the deed accomplished. Television lights that were still hot from illuminating his last Presidential address were momentarily turned off and cooled in the East Room before being turned on again for the Presidential inauguration of Gerald Ford.

The cameras self-consciously waited.

For 18 months President Nixon and the men who had been charged or indicted or tried or convicted or jailed had endured a public ordeal that transcended the deeds committed. By August, they had built up an immunity to pain, since agony had become their daily exercise.

In death the agony is over and the pain of loved ones is often surrendered to the compensation that the suffering is done. But that was not to be the destiny of August's tragedy. The public harassment and hell would be elongated for him and for others.

Inequity had already stretched beyond the realm of American justice. We allowed a criterion to be applied to President Nixon and those charged that had never been applied to others. For them, we made public judgments based on selected private conservations in which we were not participants, knowing well that few, similarly recorded, would pass such public assessment. How many intentionally forgotten smoking pistols lay in the back of closets? To judge any man on the basis of a few among thousands of private conversations was hypocritical at best and tragic at worst.

Little men, who in comparison to them, had neither the devotion nor the ability to work for all they had struggled for, were yelling for more severe penalties. Little men longed to participate in a public autopsy.

"Obstruction of justice," they said.

But did any of those who assessed and accused ask themselves how they would have reacted?

The President's closest associates and best friends who had stood by him through the very best of times and the very worst of times knew that one or more among them were possibly involved in putting "bugs" in the headquarters of his political rivals. They did not want the fact revealed, as the revelation of such an incident would likely bring about the end to everything the President had worked toward throughout his lifetime, as well as all they had worked toward during the past decade. His Presidency might be lost, the plan to end involvement in a war might be demolished, his plans for what he hoped and believed would be a structure of peace would be left to other men with whom he did not agree and whose global philosophy was anathema to his. It would be certain that some of their associates would be charged, undoubtedly indicted, and probably jailed. A nonsensical escapade in the pursuit of trifles held ruin in its revelation. In a similar situation, who would have picked up the telephone, dialed the police, looked over at friends, and said, "I'm turning you in"?

The President was a lawyer. He was not born a lawyer. He was born a human being. But the reaction of others was less than human. The President was treated as though he had committed a mass murder, and

98

his friends were treated as though they were his instruments in the dropping of hydrogen bombs.

It is a tragedy of human nature that too often we judge others by the darkness of their worst predicament while we judge ourselves in the light of our highest accomplishment.

Hypocritical men are quick to condemn, to act horrified, to discard and depose. Hypocritical men comprehend, but do not aid. They do not attempt to lift others to newer heights, but rush to bury them in greater depths.

"But he lied to the American people," they said.

He did.

The decision of nonrevelation most often leads to lying, whether it be to one or millions, as lying is the grotesque detour that waits unseen beyond the bend of nonrevelation when vigilance is maintained by others. When a man is no longer the master of events, he becomes their slave.

Lying is neither an enviable nor an excusable decision, but it is a decision that has been regrettably made by many of the best of men. It can be said that other Presidents have "covered up" for one reason or another that brought them to lie. Although they lied is not a factor for justification, it is a factor for recognition that they, like their predecessors and followers, may well have been good and decent men, but were not good and decent gods.

Honesty is a virtue. It is not the only virtue, and virtues sometimes conflict with other virtues, and principles sometimes conflict with other principles. The making of a man is the choices he makes between them and the priorities he sorts out and gathers and rearranges each day as one virtue and principle oppose other virtues and principles. Those choices are the most dangerous of thought processes, and they come more frequently as life goes on and as more objectives are met. What to one man is little more than an error in judgment at his point of life is no less than the breaking of another man at his point of life.

If it was an evil for him to lie, a greater evil was accomplished when the accepted rules of political life and Washington journalism were changed in the middle of his administration, though he had been the victim of such rules throughout his political career. The political rules and their observance by journalists not only offered acceptance of "dirty tricks", but demanded that those who discovered such tricks never expose them. He didn't reveal them when he was their victim, just as he did not when he countenanced them.

It is also worth noting that the great obscenity was done, not by the

99

President's using obscenities in private, with the expletives deleted on the transcripts, but in the exposition of those obscenities to the public.

During that period when voices yelled "Punishment to him and his fallen men!" we should have stood before a mirror and exhibited ourselves to ourselves, looking closely through that mirror all the way to our own thought processes. We should have looked at the human spirit that was meant to raise us above the animal. Some should have asked if they perceived an imminent national agony from which they wished to save the country or if they were witnessing a current drama to which they wanted to add their double standard of morality in the public spotlight. How many were hearing sirens and following their wail? How many pleasured in the tragedy of others?

All who acted horror-struck should have added consistency to that characteristic by asking God that they be judged by their thought processes and private conversations at a time of personal bewilderment and tragedy, to the exclusion of all else.

History unfortunately is recorded by historians, and for that reason future generations may not be told much about the punishment-seekers. Between pages 230 and 232 in a brown-bound history book of future students will be found the paragraphs covering those years, with the probable summary that justice was done. But what truly occurred was a series of the most blatant and ignored injustices this country prescribed since black citizens were allowed to be felled by water hoses and American citizens of Japanese heritage were contained in barbed-wire camps.

If reservations can be made for paragraphs within those brown-bound books, then space for a paragraph should be reserved to reveal that, though the so-called "Watergate" cases heavily involved partisan politics, the Watergate grand jury of 23 people had only one Republican member.

Space should be reserved to inform the yet unborn reader that the pretrial publicity of the "Watergate" case had not been exceeded by any case in the lifetime of the nation, yet the Sam Sheppard case was dropped because of the pretrial publicity, as was the case against Lieutenant William Calley. Space should be reserved to record that, in April of 1975, the murder trial of Joan Little was moved from one area of North Carolina to another because of pretrial publicity and the racial composition of the jury pool.

Space should be reserved for a paragraph to tell that what was labeled as "the Watergate trial" was conducted in the only area of the country, save one, that voted against President Nixon's reelection. The space for a footnote should be reserved to tell that the vote in the District of Columbia was 78% for McGovern compared to a national average of 61% for President Nixon, and space should be set aside to point out that the American Civil Liberties Union would undoubtedly and justifiably have protested if McGovern had won 49 states and some of his former associates were tried in the unique political zones of McGovern defeat in, let us say, Orange County, California or Meridian, Mississippi.

Space should be reserved for a paragraph reprinting Senator Sam Ervin's statement in defense of having his Senate Select Hearings televised when he granted that television coverage of the hearings would be prejudicial by stating, "The exposure of the truth is more important than putting a few men in jail." Reserve space for a sentence to state that the quotation was quickly buried after the televised Senate Select Hearings were over.

Most of all, space should be reserved for a paragraph to let future generations know that none of the national television commentators of the time even mentioned any of the inequities listed above. No David Brinkley commentaries. No Dan Rather capsulizations. No shaking head of Eric Sevareid.

The continuation of fine-printed techniques, "un-news," and the absence of diverse editorials left the public uninformed, and so Judges Sirica and Gesell found it easy to refuse justified changes of venue, easy to reject valid postponements of trials, and difficult to dismiss their own forthcoming roles in history. Immortality has always been the greatest passion of man, and to leave something behind or to be recorded in history is the only way known to achieve such immortality among men. There was no public pressure for them to rise above their own weaknesses by self-imposed rejection of their own legacies.

The television networks guaranteed that the way in which the men were to be tried would be tantamount to the actions of a lynch mob. The guarantee was kept. Earlier lynch mobs in the deep South and the far West compared favorably with those of the 1970s. The rocks used in the 1970s were shaped like microphones and portable television cameras, waiting to be wielded at the entrances and exits of the courthouse, waiting to exhibit a defendant being spat upon, while artists' conceptions were being drawn to exhibit to millions each reaction of each defendant to each piece of evidence.

The television harassment, ridicule, never-decreasing speeches, commentaries, and analyses of the previous two years were second to none. What was the difference between a vigilante haranguing a crowd in front of a saloon and David Brinkley speaking on NBC to millions of Americans? What was the difference between a self-appointed deputy addressing a township and Eric Sevareid on CBS attempting to prejudice a nation?

President Nixon and his men had accomplished much for the nation and much for mankind.

There were no personal rewards.

"Send three doctors!" one said.

"Let us play the tapes on television!" three said.

Those who had created the climate for the fall of the administration seemed bewildered for a short while after President Nixon's resignation. The only absolute defeat is the admission of defeat—and he admitted he was defeated. Their resultant bewilderment was evident in their search for stories about him. Like picadors in a bull ring, the sparkle came back to the commentators' eyes only when the dateline was San Clemente or the Washington courthouse or the Long Beach Hospital.

"Our long national nightmare is over," Gerald Ford said upon taking office as President. "May our former President, who brought peace to millions, find it for himself." But those who could bring that peace to him did not seem as steadfast and eager to accomplish it as the former President had been in his attempt to bring peace to those millions. The vision of man is obscured only by his own willingness to close his eyes; and the few who could end the nightmare refused to open their eyes and terminate that dream of anguish.

Unlike the death of a President, eulogies were replaced by subpoenas, tributes were replaced by ridicule, and the peace he so richly deserved was replaced by the rhetoric of lesser men.

9

Instant Replay

Ecstasy, like laughing and dying, comes unexpectedly and lasts a very short time.

It was that way for President Ford and his relationship with the media. It was neither a honeymoon nor a good marriage. It was an affair.

During the short period of the motel room romance, the media spent as much time talking publicly about the impotence of his predecessor as they did in complimenting the new man for his virility. You never trust a woman with that kind of dialogue.

Within weeks of the birth of Gerald Ford's Presidency, *The Washington Post* grew weary of printing photographs of economic advisors sitting around conference tables and so it ran a front-page article on San Clemente that hinted that all was not well within the compound. The story was headlined, "Nixon in Exile: Lonely, Depressed." It was noted within the story that a Secret Service agent referred to President Nixon as "the old man," but the *Post* neglected to tell its readers that the President had been informally referred to in the same terms by many on the White House staff since 1969.

Sounding more like Izvestia reporting a change of the Politburo, *The Washington Post* advocated that all Nixon appointees (except President Ford) be removed from government regardless of their innocence of any charge—in other words, a purge.

With glee, *The New York Times* published its paperback volume entitled *The End of a Presidency* while *The Washington Post* issued its competitive paperback, *The Fall of a President*. Both books included the transcript of June 23, 1972; though both newspapers had been highly critical of differences between the White House version and the House Committee on the Judiciary version of previous transcripts, there were differences in the two versions of the same transcripts printed in the *Times* and the *Post* books, even though they relied on the same sources.

Newsweek magazine, unable to print new out-of-context transcripts on its cover and unable to photograph perspiration above the upper lip of the former President, told its readers that a report from San Clemente relayed the news that Nixon had taken to wandering around his estate in need of a shave and that his clothes were rumpled. Weird. What man would do that when he has no place to go?

Time magazine, discovering that the former President made a telephone call from San Clemente, paralleled that erratic behavior with Martha Mitchell. Good idea.

Massacring President Nixon and his men was a very tough habit to break.

But for the new President it was different. He was terrific—as long as he didn't do anything that contravened their judgment. They offered praise every time he looked at a camera and smiled. They applauded his "open door" policy as a new precedent, forgetting that every new President in recent times initiated an open door, which was generally closed after a few months in the White House so some work could be accomplished. No matter. This man was not Nixon. In their wooing period, they gave him higher praise for taking his own English muffins out of the toaster than they had given President Nixon for bringing our American prisoners of war out of captivity.

David Brinkley was approaching an embarrassing height of jubilance in front of everyone as he somehow managed to favorably compare the buttering of the muffin with the "secretiveness" of Nixon. A hard comparison to grasp, but he must have known what he meant even if the viewer didn't.

Things were never better.

Then President Ford issued his pardon of President Nixon.

That did it.

The end of the affair. Goodbye. Everything. Out. Slam. Done. Not even a kiss on the cheek.

CBS went into a state of hysteria. With their usual keen sense of balance, a team of four newsmen moderated by a wide-eyed and open-mouthed Dan Rather, agreed that President Ford was really asking for it. Dan Rather referred to the pardon as a "deal" so many times that Bob Schieffer finally said:

> . . . I would just like to add one thing for the record. What the Ford people are saying for the record is that there was no deal. They say that the President made up his mind to give President Nixon a pardon. Now they admit that the decision was not announced until after Mr. Becker went out there to San Clemente and came back and said, you know, that we're going to have arrangements worked out on the tapes. But they're saying that the granting of the pardon had nothing to do with any other event, that no deal was struck with Mr. Jaworski and that no deal was struck with Mr. Nixon. I'm telling you that's what they said for the record.

Although Schieffer had couched his remarks in enough variables to satisfy the most pessimistic and suspicious critic, Rather was angry. "Well," Rather said, "what happened to the era of straight talk? I mean a deal is a deal is a deal. If they don't call it a deal, what do they call it?"

They call it a pardon.

Phil Jones, exercising the new code of journalistic illegality, that of ignoring the confidentiality of the grand jury, said:

> . . . members of the original Watergate grand jury are extremely upset by President Ford's decision. This is the same grand jury that voted earlier this year to name Richard Nixon as an unindicted co-conspirator, and the jurors would have indicted him had it not been for the legal advice from Special Prosecutor Jaworski that a sitting President could not be indicted. There was reportedly a straw vote taken by the jurors at that time. Eighteen were present, and when asked if they would like to indict then-President Nixon, most of those present held up both hands.
>
> Now some members of this grand jury are described as having hit the ceiling. Their words of reaction to the President's decision today—"outrageous, furious, baffled." One juror is quoted as saying, "The President talks about proclaiming domestic tranquility and simple justice, yet we have people in Canada who can't come home because they don't have full presidential pardon or any indication that they're going to get it." That being a reference to Vietnam draft evaders.
>
> The jurors are puzzled over whether they have any recourse, but it is known that some of them feel their indictments of other Nixon aides are totally unfair if the same justice system is not applied to Nixon. One juror is quoted as saying, "Here we sat on this case for 2½ years doing what we thought was right. Now this happens. It is worse than the way the Agnew thing was handled."

Then there were the predictions. Bruce Morton didn't think the pardon would be one of the issues of utmost importance two years later in the Presidential election of 1976, but Bob Schieffer disagreed:

> No, I think it will be one of them. I think it will be the main one. I mean the people are going to say, "This man said he would not do this, and now he's done it. How will we know that he's not going to keep his word from now on?"

This was followed by a mysterious prediction of Fred Graham when Dan Rather asked him if anyone had heard from Special Prosecutor Leon Jaworski regarding the pardon. Graham answered:

> Well, I can't—I haven't been able to talk to him, obviously. He's really done a disappearing act. But I have talked to some people quite close to him today, and one of them said what to me was an intriguing thing. I said, "Well, what do you"—meaning "you" in the plural—"intend to do about this?"
> And he said, "Well, you may know that in two or three days." And he indicated that it might be something that would happen publicly, and that's very mysterious and that's all I can say.

We are still waiting.

NBC was also inaccurately noting that there might have been "a deal" made between the former President and the incumbent President, and on the following evenings Cassie Mackin made a nightly pursuit of those in the Congress who took a critical view of the pardon.

ABC was distressed that both the impeachment and judicial processes had been cut short and, with a style reminiscent of FDR's references to Martin, Barton, and Fish, ABC repeatedly quoted all the 1974 custodians of American morality: Weicker, Schweiker, and Byrd.

The editorialists, Brinkley and Sevareid, took different views of the pardon. Brinkley was so angered that he suggested that President Ford had acted outside the law; Sevareid, being more of a realist, offered no such inaccurate assessment. Realizing the pardon was done and irrevocable, he proceeded to recommend alternate means of recrimination: the House of Representatives could continue with impeachment even though Nixon had already resigned; the Grand Jury could issue indictments against him though he couldn't be prosecuted; or the House and Senate could jointly censure him. Splendid.

From the way they talked, it didn't appear that the news organizations wanted America's long national nightmare to end or their long national newscasts to be discontinued.

Another Boredom Crisis could be enough to finish them.

Time and *Newsweek* Magazines were predictably as horrified as the networks at the nightmare's possible termination. *Time* noted:

> Ford's first major decision raises disturbing questions about his judgment and his leadership capabilities and called into question his competence. He had apparently needlessly, even recklessly, squandered some of that public trust that is so vital to every President. . . Those somewhat jesting earlier cracks about Ford's intellect were now seen in a more serious light. How could he have failed to see the ramifications—legal, political and moral—of his decision?

Newsweek noted that "all the old jokes about the President's intellectual capacity were being revived," that he "seemed to have stampeded himself into a badly timed decision," that "the White House rarely seemed to know what it was doing," and "partly in response to the administration's blunders . . . the stock market plunged fifty points last week."

After President Ford, in an unprecedented move, appeared before a subcommittee of the House to submit to questioning regarding his pardon of President Nixon, *The Washington Post's* editorial read:

> . . . The President's explanations were not much different than those he gave the first time around, and they are therefore hardly likely to be any more satisfying to those, such as ourselves, who strongly believe that the pardon was ill-timed and mismanaged. . . .

But did *The Washington Post* expect that President Ford's explanations would be different from those he gave earlier? Why should he change his explanations? (I would assume that, as an honest man, if he was asked the same question a thousand times, his answer would remain unchanged. Further, if it was changed, I would expect *The Washington Post* to be the first to call him a liar for the difference in his explanations.)

The point being missed, of course, was that President Nixon was *not* just like anyone else, and should not have been treated as an average man. The press had not treated him as an average man before; why should it now do so? A man who committed murder would not have been given years of headlines, harassment, and ridicule. (In some cases they have been given sympathy.) If President Nixon was not treated equally with others, it was because his position stripped him of that equality, for better or worse—not just for worse. Nor was this the first use of the Presidential pardon. The very existence of the pardoning

107

power in the Constitution is not, by any stretch of the imagination, a stratagem for equality, but a device for extraordinary circumstances that the President can use as he sees fit. And President Ford saw fit.

After his exercise of the pardoning power for President Nixon, one bright note remained for those who sought further recriminations. Unless President Ford issued more pardons, the trials of former Nixon associates would soon begin. The commentators would try to ensure that President Ford would not overrule their wisdom again.

The power of the media was, at this point, becoming painfully apparent to President Ford.

Rather than being perceived as the relayers of news, the most powerful news organizations had graduated to administration recognition that they were the creators of policy, and he knew he was not in any way immune from their power to influence the national pulse against him, as well as for him. Therefore, he literally asked the media if he should pardon those charged from the Nixon Administration.

They answered without hesitancy: "No."

His "inquiry of the media" led *The Washington Post* to write: ". . . as one defense lawyer in the cover-up case put it, 'If it's a trial balloon, it's the stupidest one I've ever seen. The way to float one is to leak it out, not to announce that it's been authorized by the President.' "

And so without pardons from President Ford and not having received pardons from President Nixon before he left office (a tragic error), Bob Haldeman, John Ehrlichman, John Mitchell, Robert Mardian, and Kenneth Parkinson went to trial.

But what about other people who had supported President Nixon but weren't trapped in that mouth-watering phrase, "Watergate"? What about Senator Gurney, who had been the only supporter of President Nixon on the Senate Select Committee? What about John Connolly, the Democrat turned Republican, who came back to the administration to help President Nixon when others were leaving? And what about the President's two closest personal friends, Charles (Bebe) Rebozo and Robert Abplanalp, who actually *liked* him?

Senator Gurney's Senatorial career was ended with an indictment. Governor Connolly's national aspirations were shaken with an indictment and 18 months of publicity. Both Senator Gurney and Governor Connolly were acquitted. Rebozo's fortune spiraled downward as his attorney's fees spiraled upward. And Abplanalp's aerosol spray-can industry came under siege. It was not conspiratorial, but it left President Nixon with practically all close friends in grave and unrelated difficulties.

Next was the 1974 election. It was not difficult for the media to choose the victors and losers. The media set the issues, defined the campaign criteria, and the administration accepted those issues and definitions. Without taking initiative in any areas other than the ones the national communicators advanced (which would bring defeat to President Ford's party), the Ford administration followed the media's lead and neglected to use a strong voice or initiate or veto legislation on a whole raft of controversial issues that could have established dialogue on policy, as was true in 1972. Instead, the media-inspired issue of "throw the rascals out" was the main theme.

And so the election campaigns were a breeze. CBS and NBC began their series of reports within their network news broadcasts, focusing on individual races, each with a tilt toward their favorite candidate: Brown, not Flournoy; McGovern, not Thorsness; Hart, not Dominick. On and on it went.

They succeeded in every venture except one: the New York Senatorial race of Jacob Javits against Ramsey Clark. But no one can blame them for not trying. During the height of the campaign, CBS focused on the New York race with some choice narrative lines:

> If Jake Javits is Goliath, take a look at David . . . [Clark]. . . There are those who say Ramsey Clark thinks that he is a saint. He is. He is a moralist . . . The campaign is a study in contrasts. Ramsey Clark's well-worn walking shoes are a trademark up and down the state. Somehow they seem to say he's forced to practice the politics of poverty. In fact, Jake Javits will outspend Clark by about two to one. But both of them have had trouble raising cash this Watergate year. . . . Essentially their battle is betweeen the politics of virtue and the politics of pragmatism. . . .

The only mention given the third candidate, Barbara Keating, was, "There is a third candidate in the race, the Conservative Party's Barbara Keating, to whom both Javits and Clark are virtually wild-eyed radicals. She's campaigning principally on the issues of crime and pornography. The polls say she'll get about ten percent of the vote."

On election night the network commentators mentioned the Clark defeat only in passing, and when CBS did mention it, Roger Mudd was moved to say, "We get the feeling we haven't seen the end of Ramsey Clark in elective politics." This was in glaring contrast to Carl Rowan, who told the television viewers from a Washington newsroom that "the most obnoxious spokesman of Nixon", Rep. Charles Sandman of New Jersey, was defeated.

That evening, Harry Reasoner of ABC mentioned that "some good

Republicans" had won reelection. (We had not previously known there was a definition of good Republicans and bad Republicans.) Leslie Stahl of CBS commented that one of the losers was "too conservative" for the voters in his state (though that question was not on the ballot). CBS ran an interesting replay of a vote on impeachment by the House Judiciary Committee to spotlight who on that committee had won and who had lost re-election; that was immediately followed by Walter Cronkite's announcement that all four former prisoners of war running for office had lost their elections. He then corrected himself by adding that the result of the fourth election was still in doubt. This was followed by John Hart saying that, in contrast to 1968, "the doves have won respectability and a place at the family table." Ramsey Clark didn't win that place at the family table, but John Hart neglected to mention his defeat.

The following morning *The New York Times* headline was an election-result vocabulary lesson: "CAREY WINS, 16-YEAR G.O.P. RULE ENDS; DEMOCRATS PILE UP CONGRESS GAINS; MRS. GRASSO VICTOR; JAVITS RENAMED."

Carey? He WINS.

GOP Rule? ENDS.

Democrats? PILE UP CONGRESS GAINS.

Grasso? VICTOR.

How about the Javits–Clark race? It didn't state JAVITS VICTOR or JAVITS WINS or JAVITS RE-ELECTED. And it certainly didn't state CLARK LOSES or CLARK DEFEATED. Instead, JAVITS IS RE-NAMED. Renamed? What the hell does that mean?

In the immediate days ahead, Gerald Ford went to visit the leaders of Japan, South Korea, and the Soviet Union. When he returned, Dan Rather of CBS was also back home from his own Summit Conference with Fidel Castro and he had a commentary that, of course, was not labeled as such. It was just a friendly reminder to Gerald Ford about what he had done wrong and what he should do next.

Dan Rather began by saying that "President Ford and his Orient Express have returned." (Get it? Just like the movie title. Great parallel for a summit conference.) Then he said that "President Ford spent so much time running around the country campaigning for Republican candidates and then followed so closely with the tour of the Far East that people simply added the time up and said he hasn't been around enough to really have been paying much attention to economic affairs."

But was President Ford "running around the country"? Was it a "tour"? And all what "people" added the time up? Who said he "hasn't been around enough"?

110

Rather went on to say, "All of Mr. Ford's travel means that economic decisions are being made, by and large, by the same men who advised President Nixon and in the same way." Untrue. "This is true because President Ford has not brought around him new economic advisors." Untrue. "As he is in most areas of the executive branch, the President is sticking with the people selected by President Nixon with their policies." Try to tell that to former Nixon aides who were at the D.C. Unemployment Office. "In the long run, this may or may not prove to have been a wise decision by Mr. Ford. In the short run, it does not, to say the least, lead to confidence. . . ."

Ron Nessen, the President's Press Secretary (formerly with NBC), did not at this time strike out at the media, but instead attacked his predecessor, Ron Ziegler, whenever he could for no apparent reason other than to compare himself favorably with Ziegler to the White House press corps.

The Ford administration was giving more servitude to the eccentricities and objectives of the national media than any administration in history, but it was not appreciated.

The New Year's present to Gerald Ford arrived in CBS' year-end wrap-up entitled: "1974, A Television Album" in which Bob Schieffer summed up his assessment of the accomplishments of the President: ". . . Except for the changes in style, the only thing that Gerald Ford has really been able to change so far this year is the fate of Richard Nixon."

Although Schieffer's assessment was grotesquely inaccurate and blatantly biased, Gerald Ford *had* gone out of his way to change the style from that of the preceeding administration. Since President Nixon had addressed the White House press corps from the east side of the East Room, President Ford spoke to the White House press corps from the west side of the East Room. Then he moved the next press conference out to the Rose Garden. Then he moved it to Room 450 of the Old Executive Office Building.

Since President Nixon gave his policy speeches from the Oval Office, President Ford used the White House Library.

Since President Nixon was criticized for being unseen for long stretches of time, President Ford made sure he could never be so accused.

He did everything as visually different as possible from his predecessor. (Richard Nixon could never have worn a ski outfit or a "WIN" button.) Still, it didn't work. Roger Mudd was to lavish the final insult upon President Ford when he reported to CBS' news viewers "The [Senate Foreign Relations] Committee had been irritated by Secretary

Kissinger's inability or refusal to testify, so this afternoon it got an appointment with the next best White House official, the President himself."

The media just wouldn't let the change in style fool them. Try as he might, Gerald Ford couldn't bring back the rapport he held with them in the prepardon month of his Presidency. It didn't look as though the affair could be revived.

Then at one of the press conferences he noticed the medium had a gleam in her eye. Just a quick sparkle. Still enticing. When she noticed him exchange the glance, she handed him an envelope.

After the press conference was over, he went to the Oval Office and locked the door. He opened the envelope and read the enclosed note, which permeated the room with the aroma of perfume. The note read: "Extension on amnesty. Elliott Richardson. Cuba. Busing. Kuchel. Ecology. Détente. E.R.A. Isolationism." There was no signature.

As he threw the envelope into the waste basket, something fell from the wrapper onto the floor. It was the old motel room key. He picked it up, and as he debated whether to put it into his pocket or not, he stared out the large window of the Oval Office, taking in the wide view of the South Lawn, the ellipse, and the Washington Monument. He wondered if George Washington had ever had troubles like this. Then he glanced at the flags to his left and right sides. On the left he examined the Flag of the Seal of the Presidency. He looked to the right at the American Flag. Perhaps it was his imagination, but as he glanced down at the key, then back up again, the flag looked as though it was losing color.

10

An American Surrender

The red and the blue were missing. The American flag was only white.

The document of surrender had been agreed upon 22 months before the fall of Phnom Penh and Saigon. With the finalization of that document, our flag began its slow loss of color until it was bleached by the dawn's early light of an April morning in 1975.

The American surrender would not and could not have occurred without the overlapping climates of dissent against our policy and "Watergate", fostered by our nation's prime communications arms.

The place of surrender was the United States Capitol. The date of surrender was Tuesday June 26, 1973. The document of surrender was a funding bill for agencies and departments of the United States government, with an amendment attached.

It was a case of legislative blackmail, but that was not to be the catch phrase propagated by our sources of communications. In this case, there would be no catch phrase of stigmatization.

The chronology of the document started with President Nixon's bombing raids on Hanoi and Haiphong in late 1972 that brought about the Paris peace accords and the return of our men who were prisoners of war. After those January accords regarding Vietnam were signed, President Lon Nol of Cambodia, in an effort to end the war in his country, unilaterally ceased fire while requesting a cease-fire from the 100,000

North Vietnamese in Cambodia. He asked the North Vietnamese to leave Cambodia and to stop arming the Khmer Rouge (Cambodian Communists). The North Vietnamese and the Khmer Rouge did not observe his cease-fire, which prompted him to fight back again and request more aid from the United States. President Nixon then ordered bombing of enemy targets to bring such a cease-fire about. He said the bombing would stop as soon as the Communist forces agreed to a cease-fire and the North Vietnamese returned to their borders.

Elements in the United States Congress, through a series of actions, arrived at a scheme to stop U.S. bombing with or without an agreement for a cease-fire. It also incorporated insurance that North Vietnamese violations of the Paris peace accords could not be stopped in South Vietnam, thus voiding our Presidential agreement made to the South Vietnamese. It called for an immediate halt of all U.S. military action in, over, and off the shores of Indochina: Cambodia, Laos, North Vietnam, and South Vietnam. The North Vietnamese had been brought to negotiations by the bombing raids on Hanoi and Haiphong. Without a possibility of American bombing restarting under any conditions, Hanoi would be free to do as it pleased. The amendment was attached to a funding bill for the workings of the United States Government. The only way for the President to veto the amendment was to veto the bill, which would catastrophically bring essential workings of government to an abrupt halt.

The President took the risk. On Wednesday, June 27th, with three days left before the cut-off of funds, President Nixon vetoed the bill in order to veto the amendment.

With crisis imminent, a compromise was reached between the President and the Congress on Friday June 29th. They jointly agreed that the funding of the agencies and departments of the government would continue and the amendment would be revised so that the cut-off date of military involvement would be postponed until August 15, 1973. On July 1 the President signed the bill into law.

The funding of the United States Government continued and the President had a month and a half to bring the Communist forces in Cambodia to a cease-fire. But the Communist forces knew that all they had to do was hold out until August the 15th.

They did.

The bombing stopped. When the 15th arrived the President stated: "This Congressional act undermines the prospects of world peace by raising doubts in the minds of both friends and adversaries." The resolution was to raise those doubts in a short time and to change the course of this nation and the course of many nations.

The most important date in the chronology of events that led to the end of military involvement will not be recorded in the books that trace the history of that amendment.

Monday, June 25, 1973.

One day prior to the Congressional passage of the funding bill and its amendment, Monday, June 25, 1973, there occurred in Washington an event that made the passage of the amendment possible, though preceding attempts at similar legislation had failed: the cameras and eyes of the nation were hardly focused on the U.S. funding bill. They were focused on John Dean.

He was testifying to the Senate Select Committee that President Nixon was involved in "Watergate". Dean's three-network testimony continued throughout that crucial day of legislation and until the end of the week.

Legislative blackmail was accomplished, and the United States was given a new code of conduct for one region of the world. The new code was a complete negation of the principles the United States had maintained for so many years: The United States had never offered opposition to a people—it had not even ever fought against a system. It had fought only against the expansion of a system without the consent of the people governed. But no more. Not for Indochina.

There was very little inspiration or idealism in the new Congressional code for America. There was, instead, a legalized selfishness not found in any principle upon which our society was created.

The amendment, however, was not sufficient to guarantee America's complete withdrawal from the world stage. The amendment had only singled out the four areas of Indochina. There was another phase left to the American surrender, but it could only come about if "Watergate" continued. The next phase was to be called The War Powers Resolution.

When President Nixon was at his summit of influence in early 1973, he was able to veto eight bills, with all vetos sustained through the Congress. The mandate of his reelection, the signing of the Paris Accords, and the subsequent return of American troops and American men who were prisoners of war had given him the national psychological thrust to override legislation of the Congress. But as his power eroded in the wake of charges brought against him and his Administration, the Congress enacted the second bill that shifted issues of international policy away from the executive and into the legislative branch of government.

The resolution stipulated that the President must, in every instance possible, consult with the Congress *before* any introduction of forces into areas of the world where "hostilites are clearly indicated by the circumstances". Further, the President must continue consultations with the Congress and submit, in writing, a report to the Speaker of the House

115

and the President pro tempore of the Senate within two days after sending combat-ready forces into a foreign country. He would then have to terminate all armed action within 60 days unless the Congress took other actions or unless he certified in writing that he needed an additional 30 days and the Congress concurred. There was one other item within the amendment, one that decisively moved policy matters on all international conflicts into the legislative chambers. The amendment stipulated that the Congress could *at any time* terminate U.S. hostilities abroad by a concurrent resolution, against which the President would be *deprived* of veto power. (Article One, Section Seven of the U.S. Constitution clearly gives the President veto power over, in the Constitution's words, "every bill".)

On October 24, 1973 President Nixon vetoed the War Powers Resolution, declaring that it was both unconstitutional and dangerous to the best interests of the nation.

The President said the resolution

> would seriously undermine this Nation's ability to act decisively and convincingly in times of international crisis. As a result, the confidence of our allies in our ability to assist them could be diminished and the respect of our adversaries for our deterrent posture could decline. A permanent and substantial element of unpredictability would be injected into the world's assessment of American behavior, further increasing the likelihood of miscalculation and war.
>
> If this resolution had been in operation, America's effective response to a variety of challenges in recent years would have been vastly complicated or even made impossible. We may well have been unable to respond in the way we did during the Berlin crisis of 1961, the Cuban missile crisis of 1962, the Congo rescue operation in 1964, and the Jordanian crisis of 1970—to mention just a few examples. In addition, our recent actions to bring about a peaceful settlement of the hostilities in the Middle East would have been seriously impaired if this resolution had been in force . . . [It takes] away by a mere legislative act, authorities which the President has properly exercised under the Constitution for almost 200 years. One of its provisions would automatically cut off certain authorities after sixty days unless the Congress extended them. Another would allow the Congress to eliminate certain authorities merely by the passage of a concurrent resolution—an action which does not normally have the force of law, since it denies the President his constitutional role in approving legislation.

But it was very bad timing. Only four days prior to his veto, he had discharged Archibald Cox and accepted the resultant resignations of Elliott Richardson and William Ruckelshaus. All communications to the

116

American public were immersed in what the media termed The Saturday Night Massacre and the media had little time to spend on the issue of war and peace and sacrifice and surrender. That had been their interest of the preceding decade. Not this one.

CBS gave the story of the President's veto 30 seconds, while it gave what it termed "Watergate" 17 minutes, including Walter Cronkite's interview with Archibald Cox.

NBC gave the veto story 20 seconds, while "Watergate" received 9 minutes.

ABC gave the veto story 20 seconds, while "Watergate" received 8½ minutes.

Not all of this pattern was the networks' fault. There is little to show, in a visual sense, when a President vetoes a bill. The rules of the visible and invisible were again running to the disadvantage of the national interest. But it is also true that the networks did not fight the rules to bring to their audiences the implications if the Congress were to override the President's veto. The balance of time given to the two subjects set up a priority of importance in the viewer's mind. A great national debate was avoided.

On November 7 the House of Representatives overrode the President's veto 284 to 135. Within four hours, the Senate sealed the Presidential veto's demise with a 75-to-18 vote.

The combined effect of the amendment to the funding bill and the War Powers Resolution was obvious to those who analyzed the two pieces of legislation. No longer would foreign commitments of one President be automatically honored in succeeding times. Decisions relating to the keeping of America's pledges would be in the hands of a faceless Congress. No longer could a foreign power feel secure in the word of a President and lastly in the word of a Secretary of State who represented only the President. In fact, with the passage of those pieces of legislation, no longer was the American word worth uttering. For the first time in our history there was no man who could legally speak for the country, though every other country had a chief of state who could speak for his nation. America was truly on the way to becoming a leaderless society.

At that time, few other than the President warned the nation of the implications of these two pieces of legislation.

From May of 1974 forward, with flagrant violations of the Paris Peace Accords committed by North Vietnam, the pipelines of replacements of arms and spare parts for South Vietnam were dried up. However, Moscow and Peking continued shipment of arms to North Vietnam, exceeding the one-for-one replacement ratio agreed to in the Paris Peace

117

Accords, enabling the North Vietnamese to raise the level of their combat troops in South Vietnam from 148,000 to over 300,000. When U.S. aid ran out, the Soviet Union quadrupled its aid to the North Vietnamese.

The Congress, which had demanded absolute integrity of President Nixon during the crisis that enveloped his administration during 1973 and 1974, was to abdicate integrity for the entire nation in its new-found authority. This was done by repealing the 1973 agreements made to South Vietnam.

The Paris Accords stated: "The two South Vietnamese parties shall be permitted to make periodic replacement of armaments, munitions and war material which have been destroyed, damaged, worn out or used up after the ceasefire, on the basis of piece-for-piece, of the same characteristics and properties." There was not a voice of dissent at the time.

The Congress was to disregard Dr. Kissinger's public statement of January 24, 1973: "The United States, as the President said, will continue economic aid to South Vietnam. It will continue that military aid which is permitted by the agreement. The United States is prepared to gear that military aid to the actions of other countries and not to treat it as an end in itself. . . . If for any reason the war should start at any level, it would be an unfair restriction on our South Vietnamese allies to prohibit them from replacing their weapons if their enemies are able to do so . . . This is what will govern our actions." There was not a voice of dissent at the time, and there was plenty of time for it. The initialed accords were not finally signed until 36 days after the Kissinger statement.

The Congress was to disregard the agreement of the public Joint Communique issued by Presidents Nixon and Thieu on April 3, 1973: "Both Presidents viewed with great concern infiltrations of men and weapons in sizable numbers from North Vietnam and . . . considered that actions which would threaten [the peace agreement] would call for appropriately vigorous reactions. [President Nixon] affirmed that the United States for its part, expected to continue, in accordance with its constitutional process, to supply the Republic of Vietnam with the material means for its defense consistent with the Agreement on Ending the War." There was not a voice of dissent at the time.

These were not secret agreements, but public declarations. The letters of President Nixon to President Thieu, publicized in the debate over aid in 1975, were consistent with those declarations. Some Americans easily forgot the passions of time spent. In the early days of 1973 the passion of the time was the disengagement of American troops and the return of

Americans who were prisoners of war. No public opposition was raised over the continuance of military and economic assistance to South Vietnam. There was a debate, however, as to whether the United States should give aid to *North* Nietnam if the cease-fire was obeyed by the North Vietnamese and the Viet Cong. President Nixon endorsed such aid under those conditions.

In March of 1975, as Cambodia and South Vietnam were falling, Dr. Kissinger said that if he had had any inkling that U.S. aid to American allies would be cut back, "I could not in good conscience have negotiated" the Paris Peace Accords of 1973.

General Sirik Matak of Phnom Penh wrote a letter to U.S. Ambassador John Gunther Dean on April 2, 1975, 15 days before the fall of that city, in which he thanked Ambassador Dean "for your order to transport me towards freedom," but said he would not accept the kind offer. "As for you, and in particular for your great country, I never believed for a moment that you would have this sentiment of abandoning a people which have chosen liberty. You have refused us your protection and we can do nothing about it . . You leave, and my wish is that you and your country will find happiness under this sky. But, mark it well that if I shall die here on the spot and in my country that I love, it is too bad [but] we all are born and must die [one day]. I have only committed this mistake of believing in you [America]."

General Matak was reported to have been executed three days after the fall of Phnom Penh.

There were 17 days between the Communist take-over of Cambodia and the Communist conquest of South Vietnam. President Ford had once again requested additional military supplies and economic and humanitarian aid for South Vietnam in an effort to save the country from complete defeat.

The national media were against such aid, and their propaganda campaign was put into high gear.

The New York Times front-paged a photograph of a rope around the neck of a member of the Viet Cong as a South Vietnamese seemed to be tightening that noose. Beneath the photo was the caption, "In Tan Tru, southwest of Saigon, a South Vietnamese soldier questioning a suspected Vietcong sympathizer tightens the noose around his prisoner's neck. After a beating, the civilian admitted being a scout for the North Vietnamese." NBC ran motion pictures of the same event.

The New York Times editorialized that "North Vietnam is obviously acting in massive violation of the military provisions of the 1973 truce, but President Thieu has just as clearly violated the political provisions of that accord—the procedures for establishing a coalition National Council to create a new political constitution for South Vietnam. Even now spokesmen for North Vietnam and its ally in the south, the Provisional Revolutionary Government, are insisting that their immediate goal is to implement these provisions and thereby avoid one final battle in the streets of Saigon."

The CBS Evening News of April 15, 1975 gave a report on the fighting in Xuan Loc, 40 miles east of Saigon, in which Bob Simon stated that the battle of Xuan Loc was a symbol of South Vietnam's will to resist and "a symbol of North Vietnam's determination to end the war this year, perhaps this month." Would it not have been more appropriate and more truthful to say "a symbol of North Vietnam's determination to *win* the war this year, perhaps this month"? Aggressors and defenders become blurred when one side is described as trying "to end the war". Another phrase that could have been chosen was "a symbol of North Vietnam's determination to take over all of South Vietnam this year, perhaps this month."

On the CBS Evening News of April 16, 1975 Marvin Kalb gave a report on the approaching defeat of Cambodia in which he named the cadre who would wield the real power after the imminent take-over. He said they were all fiercely nationalistic, "with bitter anti-American memories of the U.S. invasion of May, 1970, that former President Nixon called an incursion." Others might have said, "with bitter anti-American memories of the U.S. incursion of May 1970 that the North Vietnamese and Khmer Rouge had called an invasion."

Directly following President Ford's appeal for more aid for South Vietnam, CBS had a special, analyzing the President's appeal. Bruce Morton interviewed three Senators; Buckley, Church, and McGovern: a two-to-one balance. Charles Collingwood then interviewed George Ball, Zbigniew Brzezinski, and William Bundy: a two-to-one balance. Roger Mudd then interviewed Rep. Brademas, Senator Humphrey, Rep. Michel, and Senator Tower, thus providing the only two-for-two ratio of balance within the special.

Eric Sevareid suggested that ". . . there may be a number of people who really don't want to give any more military aid who will vote for a lesser sum in the expectation that there'll not be time to spend it, that this will be over anyway. They can tell their constituents they voted for it, but the result that—in their hearts they rather expected will happen, whether this is done or not . . ."

Eric Sevareid's analysis was correct. That evening the President had requested the Congress to give him a decision on the aid within nine days, by Saturday April 19, 1975. On Friday, April 18, with one day left to go before the President's requested deadline, with the issue still undecided by the Congress and with South Vietnam coming closer to defeat, the Congress went on a weekend recess to resume session on the 21st, two days after the deadline. No network analyst criticized the Congress for recessing in the face of crisis.

President Ford had also requested in his speech that Congress define his legal authority regarding the use of military troops to protect the lives of evacuees and to define his authority in that regard within the same nine days specified, by April 19.

The issue was not decided, evacuation became vital the morning of April 29, and President Ford used troops to save both American and South Vietnamese lives, a decision that was criticized since its legality was still undefined at the time. In 19 days, the Congress did not reach a decision on a matter of emergency. Again, not one critical network commentary against the inaction of the legislators.

In April 1975, as the implications of the amendment to the funding bill and the War Powers Resolution's implications were felt, as commitments were left unkept, as Cambodia fell, and as the outlook for South Vietnam was worsening, the word from all quarters was "no recriminations—no blame—no analysis. South-East Asia is the past."

South-East Asia was not the past. Unless unanalyzed laws were repealed, it was to be the lengthening shadow of the future.

That cry for no recriminations, no blame, no analysis was a call for a cover-up of many of those people and acts responsible for the fall of South-East Asia. One of the earliest to make that plea was the CBS commentator, Eric Sevareid. It was the same commentator, we remember, who had earlier suggested (in a spirit that hardly shunned recriminations) that President Nixon's impeachment proceedings should continue though he had resigned, or that grand jury indictments should be issued against him though he couldn't be prosecuted, or that the House and Senate should jointly censure him though he was out of office.

But in the face of crisis, consistency from days past to days present was difficult to find among those who deplored America's involvement in South-East Asia.

Too many of those who found compassion for the North Vietnamese suffering from American weapons of war ignored the masses suffering from the weapons of war supplied by Moscow and Peking.

Too many of those who showed resentment toward the Thieu government of South Vietnam and who had told Americans that the Vietnamese people didn't care which government had jurisdiction, ignored the hundreds of thousands of refugees streaming southward, though the border of the north was closer, and not under attack.

Too many of those who had said Americans were anti-Asian and that Americans were prejudiciously attacking Asians in North Vietnam voiced resentment when Asians from Cambodia and South Vietnam were being evacuated to the United States.

The evacuees were to hear Senator George McGovern claim that 90% of the South Vietnamese refugees "would be better off" in Vietnam, and they were to read that a California Congressman stated, "Damn it, we have too many Orientals already," and they were to read that former Senator J. William Fulbright was "no more depressed (about South Vietnam's defeat) than I would be about Arkansas losing a football game to Texas."

Our 199 years of history as a principled and unselfish nation were, at this time, no more than a memory.

South Vietnamese evacuees had many strikes against them in the United States that were not faced by immigrants from other lands. Their new home was one in which for over a decade the national media had editorialized that South Vietnam was a nation of decadence and corruption and prostitutes and pimps and drug peddlers and black marketeers and hit men and profiteers and hoodlums. Yet, as evacuees arrived in America, Elmer Lower, Vice-President for Corporate Affairs of ABC, blamed the less than cordial welcome of Vietnamese evacuees upon the United States Government, ironically stating, " . . . It seemed to me that the federal government using the mass media, as it does on many other projects, should have prepared our citizens for this new wave of immigration." It must be mentioned that Elmer Lower truly *did* welcome the evacuees to this country, but he misplaced the blame for others who did not welcome them.

Devoid of sensitivity, night after night, the networks went to evacuation camps and interviewed refugees, full face, as the refugees gave their names. The refugees, naive to the power, impact, and audience of American television, were unaware that by their public exposure they were placing their families and relatives left in South-East Asia in grave jeopardy. The refugees from Cambodia and South Vietnam were not offered the same degree of courtesy Dan Schorr of CBS had extended to the draft evader (discussed earlier) by not having his face photographed as the interview was conducted, or the same degree which would be extended to Communists in Spain by Burt Quint of NBC on May 31, 1975 by use of the same method of interview.

122

As South Vietnam was falling and refugees continued to escape, the government of the United States made contingency plans to evacuate Americans and South Vietnamese from Saigon. The contingency plans were guarded to protect lives, but were irresponsibly printed by *Time* magazine in its issue which was on the newsstands April 28th:

> . . . The Pentagon made contingency plans for an all too conceivable eventuality: the closing of Tan Son Nhut by Communist troops or the lethal SA-2 and SA-7 missiles that were being positioned near the airfield. This operation—known as Phase Two—would be carried out by more than 60 giant CH-46 and CH-53 helicopters. The choppers would whirl in from the decks of the U.S. aircraft carriers *Hancock, Okinawa* and *Midway*, now standing off South Viet Nam as part of a veritable armada of more than 40 vessels, including two other carriers.
>
> All Americans in Saigon were advised last week that the Mayday signal for Phase Two would be a weather report for Saigon of "105 and rising" broadcast over the American Radio Service, followed by the playing of several bars of "White Christmas" at 15-minute intervals. That message would send the last Americans still in Saigon streaming toward 13 "LZs," or landing zones, situated throughout the downtown district, all atop U.S.-owned or -operated buildings . . .

As defeat was close, the media's irresponsibility increased, and bias continued. On the evening of April 29, hours after the Americans had evacuated South Vietnam, CBS telecast a two and a half hour special entitled "Vietnam: A War That Is Finished," in which a chronology of American involvement was shown, tracing that American involvement through five American Presidents: Truman, Eisenhower, Johnson, Nixon, and Ford.

A President was missing.

There *was* a President mentioned between Eisenhower and Johnson on CBS' Special: it was Diem. I mention this obvious omission of President Kennedy with pride in Kennedy's commitment. Apparently CBS was not proud of his commitment and chose not to remind the audience that President Kennedy had deployed 18,000 American troops to Vietnam including the introduction of the Green Berets. The only reference made to President Kennedy during the entire two and a half hours came near the end of the production, well past the chronology, when Mike Wallace stated that President Kennedy had said that America would help, but that it was South Vietnam's war to win.

There was another sequence missing: the self-immolation of Buddhists on the streets of Saigon that was one of the major factors in the downfall of Diem as many Americans clamored for his removal—another passion of the time that was forgotten as the years went on.

A third sequence was missing: films of returned prisoners of war arriving at Clark Air Force Base. Nor was there any sequence of those returned prisoners praising President Nixon and the United States commitment to South Vietnam. Nor were there any interviews of former prisoners telling of North Vietnamese and Viet Cong tortures they underwent. There was, however, a re-run of North Vietnamese propaganda films of "well-treated" American prisoners.

There was a line missing: Charles Collingwood told the audience that after the 1954 Geneva Accords were signed, establishing the 17th parallel as the temporary division between North Vietnam and South Vietnam, the agreements were not supported by either side, a retrospect that could have included the fact that no South Vietnamese had crossed the 17th parallel to fight the North during the entire 21 years from the time the accords were signed to the surrender of Saigon on the evening of the telecast.

There were tens of thousands of amputees missing: Two young girls were chosen as the basis for a sequence illustrating the plight of amputees from the war. Of the 80,000 South Vietnamese amputees, the two CBS selected had lost their limbs, not because of the action of the North Vietnamese or Viet Cong, but because of the mistaken firing of South Vietnamese soldiers.

Within the special John Laurence reported:

The beginning of the end of American involvement became evident in the spring of 1970, as the gears of the Vietnam death machine were grinding more slowly. Four thousands Americans were to die that year; many more Vietnamese; and for the first time, Cambodians. Then days after promising to withdraw another 150,000 American troops from Vietnam, President Nixon on his own authority and without advice or consent of Congress decided to widen the war. It was time, he said, to take action, to clean out the communist sanctuaries in Cambodia. He gave his generals the authority to do what they wanted, to send some 31,000 American soldiers across the border in a final and fateful assault into Cambodia.

Huge quantities of arms and ammunition, mostly outdated or obsolete, were captured. But the retreating North Vietnamese and Viet Cong carried the war deep into Cambodia and laid the foundations for the successful struggle of the Khmer Rouge.

The intervention in Cambodia triggered sharp and strenuous protest in the United States, mainly at hundreds of college campuses, most notably at Kent State University. National guardsmen senselessly opened fire into a crowd of demonstrators, killing four students and wounding nine.

Walter Cronkite said:

> . . . We, the American people, the world's most admired democracy, cannot ever again allow ourselves to be misinformed, manipulated, and misled into disastrous foreign adventures . . .

Within "Vietnam: A War That Is Finished" the only people to emerge as heroes during the period of American involvement were the newsmen of CBS, with some praise also given to other journalists. Throughout the show CBS applauded itself, and as the program drew to a close there was a rolling title that gave screen credit to all those employees of CBS who had brought the war to American living rooms. It was an unparalleled self-tribute, particularly in view of the way the war was ending. Or perhaps that was the point.

In the issue of *Newsweek* that appeared after the fall of Saigon, a photographic history of that war was presented in an eight-page gallery. There was no photograph of the discovered graves of the Hue massacre in which 2750 bodies were found. Not even a single photograph was reprinted of any victim from Communist aggression during the entire conflict. Among the photos presented were (their captions):

"Police chief Loan executes Viet Cong, 1968." "Marine burns hut, 1965." "Victims of My Lai massacre, 1968." "GI's with Saigon whore, 1969." National Guardsmen fire into a crowd of students at Kent State, 1970." "Outside the Pentagon, antiwar demonstrators spike the guns of military police with flowers, 1967." "ARVN soldier retreats from Laos, 1971." "South Vietnamese prisoner in 'tiger cage', 1970." "North Vietnamese capture U.S. pilot, 1972." "American army deserter in Sweden, 1968." "B-52 'Stratofortress' rains bombs on North Vietnam during renewed U.S. air strikes at Christmas, 1972." "North Vietnamese hospital, 1968." "Screaming with pain, children flee misdirected napalm attack, 1972."

Time magazine stated within a "news" story:

> . . . Responding as he felt he had to, Ford has nonetheless bobbled his first grand opportunity to lead the nation out of its concentration on a lost cause and to heal the wounds of domestic partisanship over Viet Nam. To be sure, he could not with a mere speech assuage the agony or the guilt that many Americans feel when they think of the lost and ruined lives, or watch the suffering of the war victims on their television screens. The worry over what still lies ahead for those in Indochina, both Americans and those to whom the U.S. owes a moral debt of gratitude, is real enough. But something more could properly have been expected of a new Presi-

dent who had no need to feel fettered by the mistakes and the policies of the past.

Newsweek stated:

> . . . Certainly Americans are disillusioned with their Viet Nam experience, and rightly so. They are less ready to support U.S. military aid or intervention elsewhere. But that does not mean that even the collapse of South Viet Nam would turn Americans so sour on foreign affairs that they would desert their commitments in more vital areas: Europe, the Middle East, Japan and some other parts of Asia . . .

But it is not a matter of "areas", it is a matter of human beings who live in "areas". Is one human being more "vital" than another? Who decides? God? *Newsweek?*

One hopes South Vietnamese refugees in the United States were not listening to NBC's special on Vietnam in May to watch Saigon's War Memorial being toppled by the North Vietnamese as Jack Perkins of NBC said the statue was " . . . an excess of what money and bad taste can accomplish." One also hopes they did not hear Jack Perkins say, "I don't know if you call it the fall of Saigon or the liberation of Saigon."

All national communicators seemed to reflect, in the words of ABC's Harry Reasoner, that "it is now clear that we never should have been involved in Vietnam." There were others, without access to the television cameras, who felt it was clear that we should never have abandoned our word.

The amendment to the funding bill and the War Powers Resolution, enacted into law because of a bugging at the Watergate, with the subsequent pursuit and prominence it was given, were to signal a new era in the foreign relations of this country. Thus, from the most senseless acts can emerge a spark capable of igniting the world.

The expansion of that spark was felt on that last dawn of April 1975 when Saigon fell and America resigned from its platform as a world power, leaving the Soviet Union and mainland China as the dominant forces of international influence.

(11)

We
Were All
in Aspen

And so Nixon was gone and Agnew was gone and Cambodia was gone and South Vietnam was gone and American influence was gone and Laos was going and Barbara Walters was with George McGovern in Cuba. The latter two would be back very soon.

As the nations of Indochina fell, one after the other, and as nations on every continent reassessed their relationship to the United States, President Eisenhower's Domino Prophecy of the 1950s, which was debated as the Domino Theory of the 1960s, became the Domino Actuality of the 1970s.

The immediate and bold and courageous response by President Ford to the seizure of the *Mayaguez* merchant ship by the Khmer Rouge saved the nation from instant dissolution in the international community. At least we would fight for ourselves if for no one else.

But all of that is in the past. As the last days of that period engulfed us, there was an unrelated experience that could not help but be recalled from a more distant but pertinent past. The experience was one that had been shared so very often by visitors to Germany within the first 15 years following World War II. Visitors discovered that nowhere could there be found anyone in Germany who had been part of "it". Nowhere could be found anyone who had known, at the time, that "it" was taking place. During the war years, it seemed, everyone in Germany was a ski instructor far away from "it". Conscience in the postwar period was hidden beneath what appeared to be a nation of former ski instructors.

There is also good skiing in the United States.

It may help answer the questions: "Why didn't you do something to help the hundreds of thousands of refugees during the last weeks of the Cambodian and Vietnam conflicts, since all they asked for was aid and not troops? Why did you ignore so many innocent people who were to be killed in Cambodia? Why did you ignore so many innocent people who were to be killed in South Vietnam? Why didn't you keep your agreement that had led the South Vietnamese to sign the Peace Accords of 1973? When those countries were taken over, why did so many Americans resist taking the refugees, who were evacuated or escaped, into your country? What happened to the Nation of Immigrants? If you were right during the last year of that war, then weren't you wrong for the two centuries of your history past?"

"Aspen" is the answer.

Aspen is a good place. A lot of Americans live there, including the Baileys of nine chapters ago who have lived there for 15 years. And so we were with them. We spent our days skiing on the slopes and we visited the Bailey's home at night and we watched television together.

In fact, the answer is not really so bad considering that, on the Saturday night following the surrender, we sat up there watching the news that told us who was right and who was wrong. In victory, CBS, with little now to lose, threw the whole alphabet of fine-printed television techniques at the nation in one CBS Evening News half-hour broadcast. Not a special: just the day's events, excerpts from which follow:

RATHER: This country's latest super-carrier, the USS *Nimitz*, cost $692 million. That was $250 million more than planned. President Ford today officially put the monster ship into service. Robert Pierpoint was there.

PIERPOINT: The USS *Nimitz* is the world's largest warship. Shown here in sea trials, the *Nimitz* is over three football fields long, displaces 95,000 tons, takes more than 6000 men to operate. The *Nimitz* is powered by two nuclear reactors, making her the second nuclear carrier in the Navy. The *Enterprise* was the first in the fleet. Two others, the *Eisenhower* and the *Vinson*, are under construction.

THE *Nimitz* took seven years to build, cost close to $700 million, without the 100 aircraft she carries.

Today in Norfolk, Virginia, President Ford participated in the commissioning ceremonies that officially make the *Nimitz* a fighting ship.

PRESIDENT FORD: The *Nimitz* joins the fleet at an auspicious moment, when our determination to strengthen our ties with allies across both great oceans and to work for peace and stability around the world require clear demonstration.

PIERPOINT: President Ford's visit to this ship emphasizes two points: a continued commitment to a strong U.S. Navy, even when its ships like this carrier cost well over a half a billion dollars each, and a continued commitment to America's military alliances around the world, despite what has happened recently in Indochina. Robert Pierpoint, CBS News, Norfolk, Virginia.

RATHER: North Vietnam said today it is reopening its border to the South Vietnamese and said it is launching a massive reconstruction program that will give jobs to people in the South. Other reports say factories in the South are reopening.

Peter Kalischer has been traveling through the North and South to see the aftermath of the war for himself. Here is his exclusive report on Danang, South Vietnam.

KALISCHER: The Danang marketplace the afternoon the first American newsmen and one woman go on a guided tour of areas now under the control of the Provisional Revolutionary Government, which was once known as the Viet Cong. There must be 10,000 people here, more motorbikes and scooters than we saw in all Hanoi. The ESSO gas pump is smashed, but it's business as usual in jerry cans.

Dr. Thomas Hoskins of Morristown, New Jersey of the American Friends Service Committee who came to work in the German hospital two days before the take-over and stayed on.

When the revolutionary army came in and took over everything, including this hospital, what did they ask of you? What was their attitude toward you?

DR. HOSKINS: On the first day, the 29th, I was quite involved in work here, and that turned out to be the day of the take-over. The way I learned about it was I noticed that the shooting in the streets stopped at about noon, but patients began to return, staff members began to return. I didn't realize the city had been liberated, frankly, until I got in the streets that evening, saw—and seeing jeeps with citizens in them flying the liberation flag, seeing tanks coming down the street, this time driven by students, decked out in Buddhist flags. A very different scene than before.

And my first meeting with the cadres of the Liberation Front here at this hospital was when they came on Monday, I believe, and introduced themselves and asked me what I thought of the situation, and I told them.

KALISCHER: Was there anything that you could possibly describe as a bloodbath after the revolutionary army took over?

DR. HOSKINS: Nothing whatsoever, nothing whatsoever.

KALISCHER: Right now Danang has the best of two worlds, peace and stocks of American supplies abandoned by the Saigon Marines and either looted on the spot or distributed by the revolutionary army, no profiteering allowed. The dominant note is one of relaxation. The final battle has

129

been fought. For better or worse, the war is over, and how could it be for worse? Peter Kalischer, CBS News, Danang.

A report followed on City Garden Growing to Help Resist Inflation, followed by a report on the Kentucky Derby.

RATHER: Memorial observances are being held this weekend on the campus of Kent State University, where five years ago tomorrow National Guard gunfire killed four students protesting the Indochina war.

This historic week has been a time of reflection, too, for the millions who served in that war. Morton Dean reports on one veteran whose story begins in Quangtri, South Vietnam four years ago.

DEAN: He wrote and sang a different kind of protest song. In February 1971 Wayne Forbes was angry that the U.S. was not going all out to win in Vietnam.

FORBES (SINGING): I've heard veterans, soldiers say, we could end this war tomorrow; we could end it today.

DEAN: It had been a bad day for Forbes, his unit hit hard, one of his closest friends killed. Forbes was a helicopter pilot, daring, heroic—Distinguished Flying Cross, Silver Star, Bronze Star, four Purple Hearts—a hawk.

FORBES: I believed that what my small unit was doing there in the northern part of Vietnam on the DMZ was correct. We were keeping the Communists from coming south into a —into a—a democratic republic. And we were right. We were keeping the bad guys from coming south.

DEAN: And now?

FORBES: And now? I think you have to be realistic about it and say there wasn't really anything we could do about it.

DEAN: The night after Saigon surrendered, we caught up with Forbes in Abbeville, Lousiana. His views about why we fought and who was right had changed.

Wayne Forbes, hawk that I remember from 1971, traumatic change in you, . . .

FORBES: Very.

DEAN: . . . in your words.

FORBES: Very. I—when we talked I was so committed to that situation, so committed to the battle, so egotistical that I thought I could probably whip anybody that stepped up in front of me there. I was strictly hawk. But I've changed my opinion a little bit, and I think maybe the North Vietnamese won because they were right.

DEAN: That's a big change for you.

FORBES: Quite a big change. Quite a big change.

DEAN: Forbes, who had volunteered for additional duty in Vietnam, is still seeking adventure, still flies for a living, ferries helicopters to Peru where he carries oil rigs into the jungle. He says he thinks about the war frequently; it just won't go away, about what the war cost. And on this week the war ended, he thought about it some more.

FORBES: What was it worth? All of these things were—just wasted. All of my—all of my friends over there who didn't make it back were completely wasted.

DEAN: There were a lot of them.

FORBES: Quite a few. Many, many.

The audience is now shown an aerial view of South Vietnam, with a helicopter shown flying above the landscape, as we hear Forbes' music and singing:

> VOICE SINGING: Saint Peter said in Vietnam, I can tell,
> I know you'll go to heaven, son.
> You served your time in hell.
> END

Tomorrow was Sunday and a new week would start and it was time to leave Aspen. We had been up there much too long. Immersed into a pattern of thinking by those who told us how to think each night, the country denied humanity to Presidents, to other men, and then to other nations.

Inhumanity has never been an enviable disposition of man. For 15 years inhumanity had risen from a fad into our highest national priority. A thought revolution had overtaken the national conscience.

During those 15 years, the snow was very good.

Focus at Infinity

Wherever you aren't is the place you should be. In Pigalle there is a Club Miami. In Miami there is a Club Pigalle. That's the way it is in life.

The unwritten law of being in the wrong place also applies to Presidents and international conflicts. The place a President and an international conflict should not be is where they most often find themselves— in front of a camera. They cannot survive television, as it is presently constituted, for an extended period of time. Most of the best actors don't. Most of the best series don't. Not even the best commercials do. At best, they make their initial impact and start on a downward slope. Any television producer knows that, no matter how good his series and cast may be, it has a limited lifetime and must be replaced before the public sickens and tires of the series' format and its performers. Americans have a very low tolerance for seeing the same people over and over again. Just look at the divorce rate.

The only performers who have survived television with real sustaining power are Lassie and newscasters. Lassie and newscasters instinctively know all the rules of endurance. It's a matter of style. Lassie has style. With great humility she gets chickens out of mud piles, little boys out of quicksand, and she loves just to run around outside on grassy hills. She even has a very pleasant bark. She is the only dog in the history of the world who has never made a mess.

Newscasters know all the rules of endurance even better than Lassie. They, too, are there when we need them. They are at space launches and conventions and hurricanes and they rescue us from confusion by supplying their analyses to complex events that they feel are beyond the public's comprehension. The lines they say regarding an event are the lines repeated by thousands of people the following day, as though the lines were their own.

The most important rule they observe is to never make themselves more important than the events they relate. This is vital. They must convey the impression that they are messengers rather than the message itself. But they are, in reality, in the unique position of influence-peddling on a massive and unrivaled scale. They are not advocates seeking to enlist a busload of demonstrators. They are not printers of a newsletter seeking a mailing list. They are not lobbyists requesting an appointment with the administrative assistant to a congressman or senator. The nation is their audience, without appointment. They leave no phone number for later discussion or argument. They leave no calling card that identifies them as advocates of any cause. Their nightly visit is conducted in disguise: the disguise of neutrality, impartiality, and objectivity.

It has been argued that the President may appear on national television any time he desires; that he may preempt prime time to the exclusion of a major program to state his views over the airways. It *is* true the President will usually be given any television time he chooses when he is making a major address or holds a national press conference. But the President is perceived by the viewer as exactly what he is: the President, a man with a particular philosophy, the titular head of a major political party, a partisan, and one who espouses points of view with regard to any number of policies and subjects. As long as his television competitors are on prime time every night and are perceived as balanced and unbiased neutrals, the President is the loser. Unless they agree with him. Additionally, the President is not a professional television performer. Some Presidents have feared the camera. They compete with those whose careers have been spent in the pursuit of achieving professionalism in on-camera performance.

And so we are left with a nightly prime-time power that rises above that of any and all elected officials of the nation. We have seen that such a power can set the national objectives and priorities and arrange the international agenda. And in very short time.

One could pick any subject, no matter its absurdity, and network techniques could create a fact from its fiction.

Let us hypothetically assume that one network would like to reduce

134

the effectiveness of military training, another network would like to create a shortage of butter, and the third network would like to get rid of a particular administration appointee. Can these objectives be met? Easily.

Network No. 1 runs a series of reports in which newly enlisted service men are seen going through basic training: crawling through dirt, rope climbing, machine-gun practice, etc. The visual concentration is on certain men's fatigue with particular emphasis on accidents that occur during basic training.

The commentator gives figures of those who have incurred mental depression or suffered injury. One of the network reporters visits a military hospital and interviews soldiers who have been disabled during basic training. If the military officials do not permit such interviews, the television reporter simply stands outside the hospital and is photographed as he truthfully states, "At Camp Rogers, we were not allowed to photograph or talk to any of the men who lie in this hospital and are sick or maimed due to the training demanded by their military superiors."

The reports continue night after night. The military would find itself having to answer the reports, as a "no comment" would be worse. In no time at all a public debate is created.

Network No. 2 locates grocery stores where butter has been sold out. There is a report from a grocery store in Seattle, a report from another in Detroit, a report from a third store in Tallahassee, and so on. A network researcher calls up the Department of Agriculture and finds out from the Secretary's office that there is no butter shortage. The researcher calls up a number of people within the department who say they don't know what the researcher is talking about, and so don't want to say anything. That paves the way for an honest report that ". . . although the Department of Agriculture officially denies there is a butter shortage, many sources within the Department simply would not comment."

The television viewers become apprehensive, and as a precautionary measure they start stocking up on butter. The quickest way to create a shortage is to announce its existence. Within weeks the Secretary of Agriculture is "forced to admit there is a shortage of butter."

Network No. 3 follows a particular Administration appointee on a speaking tour and reports only the out-of-context and private remarks that make him sound foolish. Frequently an unflattering portrait of the appointee's face emerges on the rear screen behind the network commentator as the commentator truthfully quotes from him, then goes on

135

to the next story. In no time the appointee could be publicly perceived as a man who continually puts his foot in his mouth, with resultant public sentiment that he should be replaced by someone more responsible.

Such a power potential has no rival. Selective truths not only distort the whole, but can create collective truth from such fabrication. Those who recognize that power potential and remember the past abuses of the medium often feel that government-ordered restraints are the only answer. Perhaps a constitutional amendment. Perhaps new restrictions imposed by the Federal Communications Commission. Perhaps new guidelines for the F.C.C.'s Fairness Doctrine.

But government intervention in the activities of any communications medium is unworthy of a free society and challenges its continuing existence. It is not and should not be illegal to be biased. It is not and should not be illegal to express bias even by the use of a free society's most important system of communication.

Recognizing the unique differences between the electronic medium of communication and the printed word does, however, require new responsibilities not yet observed by the federal government, the sponsors of television programs, much of the public, and the television industry itself.

1. The Federal Government:

A. The federal government has, thus far, *limited* free expression on television rather than expanded that freedom. Often the government has misinterpreted the uniqueness inherent in television into a uniqueness it does not possess. The ban on cigarette advertising serves as a prime example of that misinterpretation. If cigarette advertising on television is harmful to the public, then *all* cigarette advertising is harmful to the public. If cigarette advertising in newspapers and billboards is *not* harmful to the public, then neither is the televised advertising of cigarettes.

The selection of a medium for advertisements of private enterprises should not be the business of the federal government. If the public's health is the issue at hand, the medium should be recognized as having no exclusivity of communications regarding that health hazard.

B. The Federal Communications Commission has become enmeshed in the area of programming while setting standards for license requirements. *All* restrictions that have nothing to do with the essential uniqueness of frequency licensing should be abolished. The F.C.C.'s 1949 report directing broadcast licensees to air views in the public interest assumes that the government will decide what views are in the public interest.

The Fairness Doctrine of the F.C.C. has defeated its stated purpose, and it has placed psychological and artificial restrictions upon an otherwise free medium. It has done so by imposing a code so restrictive that many broadcasters refrain from taking a chance on brave programming for fear of losing their licenses. Too often, the Fairness Doctrine has guaranteed either no view at all on a valuable subject or an unfair representation. Further, it has encouraged the "disguised" point of view that has been so destructive. Just as the print medium should not be restricted by the government to print only what the government determines is a "fair view," neither should the electronic medium be subject to such a dictum. The Fairness Doctrine should be discarded as soon as the television industry composes and maintains its own true code of fairness, with self-administration.

C. The equal time provision of the F.C.C. has too often ensured that the public will not be witness to a free debate, as evidenced by the occasional suspension of the rules to permit the debate of two leading candidates without participation by minor candidates. Beyond the more publicized rulings, equal time has not been the result of the provision. The watchdogging of equal time should be performed by a self-regulatory body of the television industry receiving, registering, and publicizing complaints and their resolutions, with such publicizing done on local and network news. This is another area where the government should not be involved, other than when such complaints are embodied in lawsuits.

D. With the "people's right to know" a paramount concern, a Congressional investigation of media bias should be initiated by a House or Senate select committee, with all hearings open for television coverage. The purpose of such hearings should not be to impose new government restrictions or sanctions, but to provide an out-in-the-open exposure of media practices, with the findings of the committee released to the general public.

E. The Public Broadcasting System has been financed, in large part, by the taxpayer. It has served as competition to free enterprise and has not accomplished its objectives, which were ill-conceived. Assuming that, at some time in the near or distant future, it does accomplish its objectives, the taxpayer still should not be *fined* for its continuance, as is presently the case. Despite the most able leadership of the Corporation for Public Broadcasting in the person of Henry Loomis, the theory behind having such a system within a free enterprise society has ensured its own vulnerability. Further, it makes as much sense for broadcasters who operate within the free enterprise system to advertise PBS programming as it would for General Motors to advertise Ford Motors for no cost or for

Time magazine to furnish *Newsweek* with a free page of advertising space within *Time*. This kind of "public service" is a public disservice, eroding the effectiveness of private enterprise. CPB/PBS should be financed only by taxable and nongovernmental grants. If it fails without a government subsidy, then it fails, as would any private enterprise not governmentally endowed that cannot make it in the free market place.

F. Government policies and points of view should be presented on one specified frequency or on a prescribed day and time on an hours–per–week basis on an already operating channel. By means of *sponsored* programming, this time slot or channel should be used for Presidential addresses, the President's press conferences, legislators' responses to his views, and by government spokesmen of agencies and departments. If a network chooses to run a particular piece of government programming in addition to the government time or "channel", that's the network's own business.

This device could serve many other real needs.

The government's policies could be articulated in a *creative* fashion and without programming cost to the taxpayer. Most speeches have not proven to be competitive to creative and emotional espousal of a point of view.

When CBS presented "The Selling of the Pentagon", the Defense Department did not have a comparable forum in which to present its position. The sponsor of that program had no way to tell the public that he would, indeed, present the other side. With a government time slot or channel that accepted sponsored programming only, the sponsor would be rescued.

When network news was running sympathetic filmed segments that cinematically advocated the continuance of the Office of Economic Opportunity, the administration had no competitive or creative forum in which to explain to the American people the reasons for dismantling the agency.

The Vietnam conflict needed creative explanation beyond simple speech-making to compete with the frequent visual presentations being exhibited that took a position against American involvement in the conflict.

The government time slot or channel should be operated under the auspices of the United States Information Agency, which is currently limited by Congressional act to operate only in foreign countries. The Agency's films, which are currently released world-wide, could also be exhibited on this channel for the American public.

2. Sponsors:

A. Many sponsors are spending huge sums of money for programming that is detrimental to their existence. One leading sponsor answered a viewer's complaint in the following manner:

> We decided upon the network news because, unlike specials and spectaculars, the number of viewers that we can expect to reach is fairly consistent and somewhat predictable from night to night. The [particular network's news] was chosen over [other network news shows] as the result of an evaluation by our agency of such factors as the size and composition of the audiences, as well as the relative cost efficiencies involved, which, in many cases is also a measure of the show's popularity. . . .

But are those the only factors to take into consideration? The short view may indicate an affirmative answer while the long view certainly would evoke a negative response. The ultimate success of the sponsor's product can be greatly influenced by the *point of view* the program articulates and that the sponsor *maintains* by financing the program. Sponsors should suspend advertising on shows that ultimately work against the system in which they prosper.

B. If sponsorship has *inadvertently* presented a particular point of view to which the sponsor does not subscribe, sponsorship of an alternate point of view should be standard practice. The government time slot or channel could provide the means for this.

3. The Public:

A. There is no more important element in network programming than the public. Public *awareness* of *what* is being viewed and heard and *how* the public responds to it are the final arbiters of future programming. When bias is recognized, the *sponsor* should be notified, with a copy of the letter sent to the network and local channel.

B. The content of a letter of complaint is more important than simply a letter stating that bias is recognized. Those who feel that a particular program is unfair should make known to the sponsor that they will purchase his competitor's product. Since private enterprises that have the finances are inclined to sponsor those programs that are the most widely viewed by potential customers, those who complain about the programs should either make known to the sponsor that they will discontinue viewing the program or will continue to watch the program

139

only to determine what products *not* to buy. Enough public response that *carries out* what it articulates within the letters of complaint can be a forceful factor in future sponsorship.

C. Become shareholders in the networks and be able to voice complaints to other shareholders, participate in shareholders' meetings, initiate shareholder resolutions, and vote on resolutions. Mr. Reed Irvine, the courageous chairman of Accuracy In Media Inc., has taken the lead in this direction and his impact has been highly constructive.

4. THE TELEVISION INDUSTRY:

A. The present lack of self-regulation and self-discipline guarantees self-strangulation. In a once similar circumstance, the largest studios within the motion picture industry established the Motion Picture Association of America, with a code that met the needs of the industry within a framework of responsibility and that created a forum between member companies, the government and the public. Under the Motion Picture Association of America, the motion picture rating system was also established to serve as a voluntary method of self-discipline. The MPAA has often saved the industry from having the federal government place restrictions of its own upon the industry. A *real* television code expressly addressing the matter of disguised bias is urgently needed.

The National News Council, as a means of arbitrating bias charges, is obviously not the answer, since no one pays any attention to it, it is a self-appointed body, it is not of the news organizations' making, and its ethics in the past are more than questionable.

B. Monopolization should be addressed *within* the industry and countered with solutions of the networks' own chosing. When motion picture companies ignored their own monopolization of exhibition rights, they soon suffered from government dictates. Before the government stepped in, "block booking" was the rule of the major studios that also owned major chains of theaters. As an example, motion picture theaters were *forced to buy* the worst MGM films in order to get the best. The networks are now close to engaging in that same practice, and it is only a matter of time until the system is broken in one way or another. A truly effective self-regulatory body for all these matters is long overdue.

C. End the geographic and creative plagiarism. Television is the only art form that thrives on copying. Too many television shows look the same and sound the same—series as well as news shows. This plagiarism has disintegrated to the point where each network holds the same thought patterns as its competitors. When Dwight Chapin reported to

140

court, both the CBS and NBC morning news shows used the same sentence to open their coverage: "The man who used to arrange the President's appointments has an appointment himself today." This identical thought process is symptomatic of the sameness syndrome that results from a lack of individualistic creativity.

D. Networks should either take pains to hire staffs of diverse political views or throw off the disguise of neutrality. It would serve the national interest if commentators would appear forthrightly and even proudly in the clothes that fit them best rather than the masquerade costumes that fit them poorly and, in turn, misguide their audiences. "Straight" reporting is a misnomer that protects bias with a heavy armor. Throughout most of American history the press went undisguised, and a point-of-view was then presented within a framework of ethics, resulting in instant, knowledgeable evaluation by those it serviced. One method of taking off the disguise is for television network news to present its own "celebrities" *as such.* Bill Paley, Julian Goodman, and Leonard Goldenson are three of the most influential men in the country, yet how many times have they or any network official appeared on "Meet the Press" or "Issues and Answers" or "Face the Nation" to present to the public *their* views? Not once. In addition, commentators and reporters have become national figures, yet they are not treated as such by their peers. When Daniel Schorr of CBS made a speech in Rochester, New York on November 5, 1973, it went unreported except in *The Rochester Democrat Chronicle.* But it was a newsworthy speech given by a newsworthy person, and it gave keen insight into his thinking, of which the national audience should have been informed:

> ... Anyone who cast his lot with Nixon after 1962 had to be some kind of nut. ... When you're down to 27 percent [as occurred in a 1973 poll], you're down to almost nothing considering the number of people in this country who are uninformed. ... This past year, a new kind of journalism developed, and I found myself doing on a daily routine some things I would never have done before. There was a vacuum in investigation, and the press began to try men in the most effective court in the country. The men involved in Watergate were convicted by the media, perhaps in a more meaningful way than any jail sentence they will eventually get. We've gotten good at uncovering those stories we shouldn't be covering at all. Luckily, most of what we reported turned out to be true. I'm proud. Yes, I'm happy. No. We ought to withdraw from it as soon as possible.

Walter Cronkite is even more of a national celebrity than Schorr, but the networks, not regarding him as a celebrity whose views should be

141

exposed, did not report his remark concerning the American Security Council's accusations of CBS' bias regarding matters of national defense: "There are always groups in Washington expressing views of alarm over the state of our defenses. We don't carry those stories." Nor did any network report his answer to the question he was asked regarding his salary: "I don't like to go into that. I don't think there's any reason for public knowledge. . . ." Nor did any network report his remark that ". . . I'm proud of those [newsmen] who have the courage to expose the culpable even when they might hurt the innocent. . . ."

Networks seem to be uninterested in the private viewpoints of their own commentators. Although Schorr and Cronkite are more widely known national figures than most cabinet officers, *their* activities, *their* speeches, and *their* sentiments are ignored.

It isn't that all television newscasters are worthy of our ongoing attention. Did you ever notice that, in all the published White House memos of the Nixon Administration not one attacked Eric Sevareid? It's time to confess why that is true.

It was not that we agreed with Eric Sevareid. We rarely agreed with him. It was just that we were scared because he looked and dressed exactly like God, except for his neckties. During the Vietnam-"Watergate"-Vietnam era, he cleared his throat just the way God cleared His throat. They both combed Their hair back the same way. We must also consider the fact that during that period no one knew when Eric Sevareid was born. No one remembered life before he came to this planet. No one knew anything about what he did at home—or even where his home was located. No one knew where his studio desk had been placed. Was he sitting next to Walter Cronkite, or was he in the next room, or where? Why wasn't his desk messy like David Brinkley's? All we knew about Eric Sevareid was that the camera found him when it was the right moment and left him at the proper time. It was all very mysterious. He didn't eat at Sans Souci when he was in Washington. Maybe he didn't eat at all.

There is no question about it. If the government, the sponsors, the public, and the television industry itself don't do something about future Schorrs and Cronkites and Sevareids, then Presidents and foreign commitments will just have to go on competing with all of them. But it's tough competing with collies and gods.

Epilogue: Retrospect and Coming Attractions

Once, Christians of Rome were brought to the doors of lions' dens, the doors were opened, the Christians were eaten, and crowds watched.

Once, patriots of France were brought to guillotines, the blades were dropped, their heads fell into baskets, and crowds watched.

Once, black men of America were tarred and feathered, ropes were mounted to branches, the black men were hanged, and crowds watched.

Some in the crowds enjoyed the spectacle of public punishment with secret relief that the injustices of their time passed them by and fell on others. Some enjoyed it so much that they would come from their homes again and again to mass at an arena or a courtyard or a tree. Some stayed in their homes, unable to find amusement in tragedy.

Today no journey is required to witness such a spectacle. Through antennas on rooftops, each residence is given a private view of arenas, courtyards, and trees. The 21-inch throne of injustice poses as a more civilized window than those used previously, but public humiliation and execution can still be both its intent and result.

In the early 1970s we watched Lowell Weicker sitting in the grandstand above the arena, Walter Cronkite punishing the untried in the courtyard, and a partisan prosecution staff posing for artists' conceptions around the tree.

Appointees of the elected government fell one by one, until our win-

143

dow was cleaned and made ready for the elected official himself. For him, it was limb by limb.

The window was cleaned again for the millions of Cambodia and Vietnam.

But history has always been a sad story of repetition. We all know that small unprotected countries were destroyed by their adversaries and that the most advanced civilizations of mankind were destroyed by suicide. They left their monuments in ruins for future generations to discover, examine, and conclude that it would never happen again. It always happened again.

Those civilizations were great, but they were not perfect. Perfection demands a self-respect impervious to the pursuit of self-destruction.

In the 1940s it seemed as though America might be the country headed on a path toward perfection. We were winning victories over the expansion of foreign dictators, and offering to heal the wounds of others, friends and enemies alike. A powerful and generous nation, the United States became the idol of the world. We were a very proud people. And then we examined the weapons we had laid down and pointed them at ourselves.

In the 1950s we became self-conscious of our wealth and ashamed of our power. Pride transformed to apology. We were not perfect, but while the best of America concentrated on correcting our imperfections, others devoted themselves to advertising our defects to the world, so other nations would feel increased pride in their own societies and stop comparing theirs to ours. We mistook self-consciousness for humility, and the world was disappointed in us.

In the 1960s our self-consciousness was transformed to self-flagellation, as is always the case. We went on to damn ourselves through the streets of our cities. And when our damning was done, we set the streets on fire. Later in the decade, one weapon of suicide became more advanced, more deadly. The weapon was instant false communications. We were told and came to believe that fighting for freedom for others was no longer worthwhile, that *we* were no longer worthwhile—and we believed those voices. Our progress toward equality for black citizens and our pursuit of freedom for Asians was lost by spotlighting, not the truth of our deeds, but the falsehood of our communicators' views.

The culmination occurred in the 1970s just the way it did in times past. The nonelected became more powerful than the elected. With the will of the people circumvented, the communication system became the instrument of the *coup d'état*, as it always has, and public punishments and executions were carried out, as all past and once great civilizations always have done. Then, when foreign countries were falling and cried out, we ignored their cries, their anguish, and their deaths.

In the 1970s we heard the lions roar, the blades fall, and the branches creak for many men and nations. By the false use of the First Amendment's shield our 21-inch window was guilty of negating much of the rest of the Constitution and its very purpose for being.

No true historian can feel that our country is immune from the fate of other nations in other times. Although Americans have never elected a dictator, dictators have never been freely elected in any country. They came to power through their own molding of public opinion and psychology and force.

If our civilization should ever end, future historians will not find the weapons of its destruction among the fallen pillars of the White House or the Capitol or the Supreme Court. They will need to search for the suppliers of prejudice that armed the millions of fallen antennas resting on the rubble of rooftops.

Index

149